TORONTO
IN ART

GEORGE BOYER
Downtown, 1983
oil on board
60 x 65 cm.
Kaspar Gallery

TORONTO IN ART

150 YEARS THROUGH ARTISTS' EYES

EDITH G. FIRTH

Edith G. Firth

March 6, 1984

Published by Fitzhenry & Whiteside
in co-operation with The City of Toronto

TORONTO IN ART

© City of Toronto 1983

Published by Fitzhenry & Whiteside in co-operation with the City of Toronto
in celebration of the 150th anniversary of the incorporation of Toronto as a City, 1834-1984

All rights reserved. No part of this book may be reproduced in any way without
written permission from the publisher.

Editing: Margaret E. McKelvey
Design: Sandra Meland/Word & Image
Production: Ian Gillen
Typesetting: Colborne & Cox
Colour separations and film work: Graphitech
Printing: Ashton-Potter
Binding: T.H. Best Printing Company

Printed and bound in Canada

Canadian Cataloguing in Publication Data
Firth, Edith G., 1927-
    Toronto in art
Includes index.
ISBN 0-88902-712-9 (bound)   ISBN 0-88902-723-4 (pbk.)
1. Toronto (Ont.) in art – History.   2. Toronto (Ont.) – History. I. Title.
N6547.T67F57 1983   704.9'499713541   C83-099013-5

CONTENTS

PREFACE

"Such a tame subject," it was called in 1850, and yet through the years Toronto has been portrayed by a great many artists. This book contains reproductions of more than one hundred and seventy paintings, watercolours, drawings and prints of the city, from its incorporation in 1834 right up to the present. It is not an illustrated history of Toronto, but rather a gallery of pictures with an explanatory text – a record of a century and a half of Toronto as seen through the eyes of successive generations of artists.

This is one of two official books published to celebrate the 150th anniversary of the City of Toronto. The project was co-ordinated for the Toronto Sesquicentennial Board by its Publications Committee, chaired by the City Archivist, Mr. R. Scott James. No similar book about Toronto has ever been produced, although there are many published collections of photographs of the city, both contemporary and historical, as well as a few books illustrating an individual artist's impressions of Toronto.

When the book was commissioned, several general guidelines were established. Only pictures of the City of Toronto were to be included, and there were to be no portraits. Emphasis was to be given to unfamiliar pictures; well over a hundred of those finally included have never been reproduced before. Illustrations from books and periodicals were to be used as little as possible; of the half dozen that are included all are from very rare nineteenth-century sources and only two have been reprinted in this century. The book was to be divided into five chronological sections, each with a brief historical introduction. The text accompanying the pictures was to comment on their subjects rather than on their artistic merits or significance.

When work began, it became apparent that there were literally thousands of suitable pictures in archives, libraries, art galleries, and corporate and private collections. It was necessary to choose from this embarrassment of riches, striving for a chronological, geographical and topical balance, while at the same time representing as many artists, styles and techniques as possible, all this without sacrificing artistic quality. Obviously this goal could not be achieved completely. Some parts of the city and some aspects of its life are not well represented, because appropriate pictures could not be found. In the earlier period particularly, some pictures of great historical importance have little artistic merit.

One hundred and thirty artists are represented in this book. Among them are many famous painters, draftsmen and printmakers, whose pictures of Toronto are sometimes not typical of the main body of their work. The portrait painter looks out of a window towards Osgoode Hall, the painter of the American bison stands at the mouth of the Humber River, and the Western Ontario regionalist is transfixed by the Don Jail. The big names are here, but there are also less well-known artists, as well as amateurs whose enthusiasm was sometimes greater than their talent. Together they have given us a vital record of Toronto, as it was and as it is.

Many people have provided valuable assistance during the course of the work. Some of them spent hours discussing the whole project and making extremely useful suggestions, while others miraculously produced an essential piece of information at the precise moment when I was about to abandon a hopeless quest. To all of them I am most grateful. I am particularly indebted to Professor Anthony Adamson, Professor William Kilbourn, Mr. Ian Montagnes, Mrs. H. E. Neal, Mr. Donald Ritchie, Mrs. M. W. Ross, Mr. and Mrs. Fred Schaeffer, Mr. Austin Seton Thompson and Sister Mary Bernita Young. Mr. Stephen Otto was a constant source of information, advice and encouragement. The editor, Miss Margaret McKelvey, helped from the very beginning until the last revision of the final proof. As always, the staffs of the Metropolitan Toronto Library, particularly the Canadian History and Fine Art Departments, and of the Edward P. Taylor Reference Library of the Art Gallery of Ontario were unfailingly patient and helpful.

Two groups of people were extremely important in the search for pictures – the art dealers and the curators of public collections. All of them readily understood my problems and willingly shared their knowledge with me. Among the dealers, I am especially indebted to Mr. Blair Laing, Mr. Jack Wildridge of the Roberts Gallery, and Mr. Avrom Isaacs. From the public collections, I remember with gratitude Mrs. Mary Allodi of the Royal Ontario Museum, Mr. John Crosthwait of the Metropolitan Toronto Library, Miss Pamela Wachna and Mr. Glenn Gunhouse of the Market Gallery of the City of Toronto Archives, Miss Margaret Machell and Mr. David Wistow of the Art Gallery of Ontario, Mr. Kenneth MacPherson of the Archives of Ontario, Mr. Hugh Halliday of the Canadian War Museum, Ottawa, and Mrs. Joan Murray of the Robert McLaughlin Gallery, Oshawa.

This book would not have been possible without the whole-hearted co-operation of the pictures' owners, both individual and institutional. Some have preferred to remain anonymous. To them as well as to those whose names appear with their pictures I am deeply grateful for graciously showing me their pictures, allowing them to be photographed, and giving permission for their reproduction in this book. I am grateful also to those whose pictures I was shown but was unable to use because of the necessity of achieving a balanced selection.

One of the most rewarding aspects of my work has been the kindness and enthusiasm of the artists or their families. They have readily given permission for the reproduction of their works, and have made many valuable suggestions about other possible sources. I am indebted to them for smoothing my path in many ways. Although great efforts have been made, I regret that in a very few cases it has been impossible to locate the artist's heirs. To all the artists who have portrayed Toronto, everyone interested in the city must be grateful. In a very real way, this is their book.

EDITH G. FIRTH

TORONTO
IN ART

WE WAS BORN A BRITISH SUBJECT/1834-1867

CHAPTER ONE

"We was born a British subject," wrote William Lyon Mackenzie in 1827, and "we would wish to die one."[1] Toronto's first mayor may have temporarily changed his mind – after all he led an armed rebellion ten years later – but eventually he returned to the allegiance of his birth and died as he had wished. Like Mackenzie, most of the nineteenth century citizens of Toronto were British in origin and sentiment. So also was their city.

Modern Toronto was founded in 1793 by Lieutenant Governor John Graves Simcoe as the temporary capital and naval arsenal of the new province of Upper Canada. It was a tiny, isolated outpost of empire, proudly flying the British flag in the wilderness. When it was captured by the Americans in the War of 1812 it was still only a village, separated from its fortifications by more than a mile of bush. In the late 1820s, however, the floodtides of immigration flowing up the St. Lawrence swept into the little town; it "obtained its impetus, and must go bounding on to prosperity with a rapidity nothing can arrest."[2] On March 6, 1834, Simcoe's town of York was incorporated as the City of Toronto.

The new City had a population of 9254 people, most of them recent British immigrants. In the beginning the majority came from England, but extensive Irish immigration followed the famine years of the 1840s, so that for at least thirty years many more people in Toronto were born in Ireland than in any other country, including Canada. Toronto, however, was no Boston, because more than half its Irish were Protestant. In 1834 most of the population lived south of Queen Street between Peter Street and the Don River. King Street was lined with shops, some of them developing a thriving wholesale trade with shopkeepers in the surrounding countryside. Although there were some larger establishments, industry was represented by craftsmen employing a few helpers in small workshops.

As the capital, Toronto had a preponderance of government officials and civil servants; as a burgeoning commercial centre it had many merchants and clerks. Such tradespeople as plumbers, paperhangers, lapidaries and truss-makers were able – or at least hoped – to make a living. In the 1833-34 directory, however, no one listed his occupation simply as artist or painter. The man who was to become Toronto's most famous early artist is disguised as "Cane, Paul, Coach, Sign and House-painter." In the 1837 directory, John Craig, who among other things designed the seal of the City, is listed as a "Portrait, Fancy & House Painter."

It was not until the 1840s that the profession of artist began to develop in Toronto, and even then very few were able to support themselves solely with their brush or pencil. Many of the early artists were engineers or architects. John Gillespie worked for the lithographer Hugh Scobie, as well as undertaking other commissions: in 1851, for example, the Consumers' Gas Company paid him three dollars for "an allegorical picture"[3] used in the illumination of St. Lawrence Hall for Jenny Lind's concerts. Others earned their living in unrelated fields, while talented amateurs, both residents and visitors, followed in the footsteps of Elizabeth Posthuma Simcoe, whose watercolours depicted the beginning of British settlement.

Portraits were especially in demand before photography became relatively common, and were the early artists' most lucrative source of income. Other popular types of paintings were European landscapes and copies of European pictures. In July, 1834, the new Society of Artists & Amateurs held the city's first art exhibition; almost all the 196 entries were in these three categories. As the *Patriot* put it, "The Honorary President Capt Bonnycastle shines in the ruins of Tintern Abbey."[4] This emphasis continued throughout the period. Even when the city's artists portrayed Canadian subjects they sometimes ranged far afield; the call of the wild that was to be so alluring to later Toronto artists led Paul Kane and William Armstrong to paint the Canadian West.

A surprising number of early paintings, drawings and prints of Toronto survive. Streets and buildings were portrayed by professionals and amateurs alike, while prints from some of these views were sold for a few shillings each. Before Confederation the most popular subjects were University College and the old blockhouses north of the city, painted romantically in the European tradition by, among others, the governor general and the president of the university. In the 1850s there was a vogue for panoramas of the whole city, despite what the *British Colonist* called "the difficulty of making a picture out of such a tame subject."[5]

While the artists were recording Toronto, the city itself was rapidly growing, and was achieving commercial dominance over the entire province. By 1867 the city's population was over fifty thousand people, with more than ninety-five per cent of British origin. Settlement had spread northward to the city limits at Bloor Street and westward to Christie Street, but Toronto was not yet solidly built up. "You often have to drive for miles to pay a visit in it, and many of the public institutions appear to be quite far out in the fields. The inhabitants are scattered over a vast space, and their dwellings are often separated by great town deserts...All the houses in Toronto look quite new, and you see young ones springing up like mushrooms on all sides."[6]

Although the proprietor of *The Times* thought Toronto in the 1860s "about as dull and uninteresting a place as I ever saw,"[7] one of its correspondents wrote, "The city is so very surprising in the extent and excellence of its public edifices that I was fain to write to an American friend at New York to come up and admire what had been done in architecture under a monarchy, if he wished to appreciate the horrible state of that branch of fine arts under his democracy. Churches, cathedrals, market, post-office, colleges, schools, mechanics' institute, rise in imperial dignity over the city."[8] Most visitors were impressed; a Scotsman wrote, "Toronto boasts a museum, a university, a garrison, a review, shops worthy of Glasgow, banks, busses, statues, gardens, and railways, telegraphs, steamboats, all the newest and best paraphernalia of a rich flourishing new town."[9] In 1867 Toronto was "bounding on to prosperity," just as had been foretold.

Before the age of railways most people first saw Toronto from the water, as their boat entered the harbour. They were usually unimpressed; after all, they had just seen the picturesque grandeur of Quebec, or the bustling vitality of New York. Toronto, despite the rather brash local pride of its residents, looked flat and dull, straggling narrowly along more than a mile of low shoreline. The most famous early description of the city is Mrs. Anna Jameson's: "A little, ill-built town, on low land, at the bottom of a frozen bay."[10] At the eastern edge of the city stood the windmill of Worts and Gooderham, used as a surveyors' landmark for many years. James Worts arrived in 1831, and immediately began to build a windmill like those of his native East Anglia. He was joined by his brother-in-law, William Gooderham, a year later. In 1833 Worts and Gooderham started to convert their gristmill to steam, a more efficient source of energy than wind in Toronto. Worts drowned himself in the windmill's well in 1834 following his wife's death in childbirth; Gooderham carried on alone until 1845 when he was joined by Worts' son in the firm of Gooderham and Worts. In 1837 Gooderham began a distillery in connection with the mill. Toronto's first professionally trained architects, Thomas Young and John G. Howard, both produced pictures of the new city. Young prepared a set of four drawings – this general view, and views of King Street, Upper Canada College, and the Parliament Buildings – which were sent to Nathaniel Currier in New York for lithographing. Although the prints were advertised for sale in May, 1835, when Currier was just starting his business, they were not ready until a year later. In the 1850s Currier joined J. M. Ives to form the firm of Currier and Ives.

THOMAS YOUNG
General view of the City of Toronto, 1836
lithograph on stone by J.H. Bufford,
Published by N. Currier, New York
30.3 x 45.3 cm.
ROM SS

UNKNOWN ARTIST *Powell shooting Anderson*, 1839 woodcut 7.8 x 9.8 cm.
W.L. Mackenzie, *The History of the Battle of Toronto*, 1839 MTL

POWELL SHOOTING ANDERSON

In December, 1837, Toronto's first mayor, the radical William Lyon Mackenzie, led a rebellion against the government. His little army, consisting mainly of York County farmers, gathered at Montgomery's Tavern on Yonge Street north of the present Eglinton Avenue, then some distance from the city. Ill-organized, ill-armed, and ill-trained, they had little chance of success. On the night of December 3, a reconnaissance party led by Mackenzie met Alderman John Powell and Archibald Macdonald coming up Yonge Street from the city on a similar mission. Powell and Macdonald were taken prisoner. On their assurance that they were unarmed they were escorted back to Montgomery's Tavern by two men; one of them, Anthony Anderson, was one of the few effective rebel military leaders. As they approached the tavern, Powell produced a pistol and shot Anderson. On December 7 the rebels were easily defeated; Mackenzie fled to the United States where he lived in exile until 1850, and Samuel Lount and Peter Matthews were hanged in front of Toronto Jail. Powell was elected Mayor of Toronto for the next three years. Mackenzie wrote his account of the rebellion for a Watertown, N.Y. newspaper; in 1838 it was published in Toronto with editorial comments by a government supporter, Charles Fothergill, and an appendix by Powell, under the title, *Mackenzie's Own Narrative of the Late Rebellion*. The pamphlet was reprinted in Rochester in 1839, with the title, *The History of the Battle of Toronto*. This woodcut on the title-page of the Rochester edition was probably printed from a vaguely suitable block that the printer had on hand, but may have been especially prepared – by an artist who had never seen Toronto.

JOHN GEORGE HOWARD *Parliament Buildings*, 1834 watercolour 33.7 x 50 cm. THB Colborne Lodge

PARLIAMENT BUILDINGS

The third Parliament Buildings, erected 1829-32 from the designs of Thomas Rogers, stood on the north side of Front Street between Simcoe and John Streets. They were not universally admired. Walter Henry wrote, "the Parliament House, built of brick, looks very heavy; and has a deep and disproportioned cornice – somewhat after the fashion of a grenadier's cap on a child's head."[11] Mrs. Jameson went further, describing them as "built of staring red brick in the most tasteless, vulgar style imaginable."[12] The buildings were used by the government of Upper Canada until the union of Upper and Lower Canada in 1841, when Toronto lost its position as capital. From 1849 to 1851 and from 1855 to 1859 they were used by the United Province of Canada, and from Confederation until 1892 by the Province of Ontario. They were demolished in 1900. On the left of the Parliament Buildings can be seen the immigration sheds and the Greenland Fisheries Tavern. The creek rose near the present corner of Markham and Harbord Streets, and is typical of several small streams that ran through the city.

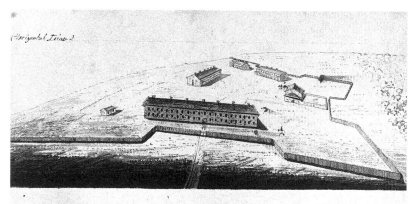

After the Rebellion of 1837, Fort York was superceded by the New Fort, in the present Canadian National Exhibition grounds. Thomas Glegg, who may have been involved in its construction, wrote, "The New Barrack Establishment was began in Feby 1840 – and completed in October 1841 – The exterior walls are of coursed hammer dressed stone from the quarry at Queenston – the whole is well drained & is surrounded by a picket fence 8 feet high. As a Barrack it is complete in every respect having every desirable accommodation. – It is situated about ½ mile from the City west-ward on the banks of Lake Ontario. It is calculated for 300 Men. The total cost about £19000 Sterling."[13] In 1893 the New Fort was named the Stanley Barracks after Lord Stanley, then governor general. Starting in the 1930s the buildings were torn down one by one, until by 1953 only the officers' quarters remained. It is now used for the Toronto Historical Board's Marine Museum.

WEST VIEW OF THE CITY OF TORONTO

Toronto's main street throughout most of the nineteenth century was King Street, shown here looking west from the present Victoria Street. In 1840 a British soldier wrote that "King Street is the great thoroughfare of the Town. The houses are principally built of brick and have their lower stories for the most part laid out in shops. This handsome street is however, as is the case in all American cities, disfigured by an intermixture of mean wooden buildings with the more substantial edifices erected on the surrounding lots."[14] Gillespie was noted for the accuracy of his views of Toronto; the *British Colonist* said of one of his paintings that "not a building nor a chimney will be found out of its place."[15] F. C. Capreol, the publisher of this print, was a local auctioneer and real estate agent who later became well known as a railway and canal promoter. The impression reproduced here has had some of the shop names altered, and numbers added referring to a key to the picture.

THOMAS GLEGG
Bird's Eye View of the New Fort at Toronto,
Upper Canada, 1842
pen/ink/wash
7.9 x 18.4 cm.
AO Thomas Glegg, "Sketch Book, Note Book"
1841-42

JOHN GILLESPIE
West View of the City of Toronto, 1842
lithograph with one tint stone, Dodson lith.,
Day & Haghe lithrs, London, published by
F. C. Capreol
32.1 x 62.1 cm.
MTL JRR T12598

JOHN GEORGE HOWARD *Toronto Bay*, 1835 watercolour 32.5 x 43.2 cm. THB Colborne Lodge

TORONTO BAY

On Christmas Day, 1834, Toronto Bay froze over; the ice remained until March 29, giving the inhabitants their usual winter playground and their source of ice for refrigeration. In the early years skating and sleighing were the most popular sports, but in the last half of the nineteenth century iceboating was the rage, with the harbour police patrolling in their own iceboat. Hockey and curling matches were also held, while hawkers took their braziers onto the ice selling baked potatoes and roast chestnuts. By the 1920s the city's heat, the water's pollution and icebreakers kept the bay open, but one year in the early 1940s the bay froze solid again. Skating and iceboating were again enjoyed, with dangerous areas marked off by discarded Christmas trees, just as trees had been used in the 1830s. This view shows the shoreline from the Garrison to the Parliament Buildings on the western edge of the city. The Fort was originally built by Lieutenant Governor Simcoe, but it had been seriously damaged in the War of 1812, so that the buildings shown here date from the war or shortly after.

JOHN GILLESPIE *View of King Street, Toronto*, 1844/45 oil on canvas 27.9 x 55.9 cm. ROM SS

VIEW OF KING STREET, TORONTO

Although Mrs. Mary O'Brien thought that Toronto was "so scattered that I hardly know where the centre may be,"[16] this part of King Street west of Jarvis Street was the focal point of the early city, with the Market/City Hall on the south, St. James' Cathedral on the north, the Court House (not shown) around the corner on Church Street, and many of the principal shops. Toronto streets were first lit by gas on December 28, 1841, "a novel and brilliant spectacle."[17] Before Toronto was incorporated, its municipal affairs were administered by government-appointed magistrates meeting in the General Quarter Sessions of the Peace. They were responsible for the building of the

Market in 1831-33, designed by James Cooper, at a cost of more than £9000. This then enormous debt influenced the Tories to support incorporation with its increased taxing powers, a position already held by the radicals who wanted a more democratic local government. The Market, standing on the present site of St. Lawrence Hall, was a large building around an interior courtyard onto which opened the butchers', greengrocers' and farmers' stalls; above the stalls were offices and meeting rooms. The first city council chambers and municipal offices were upstairs in the taller central section on King Street. The front portion of the building was destroyed in the Great Fire of 1849.

ATTRIBUTED TO JAMES HAMILTON
Moss Park, 1842
pen & ink
26.8 x 42.2 cm.
MTL JRR T11096

MOSS PARK

William Allan was probably the most successful businessman in the town of York – he was the financial brain of the Family Compact. In 1828 he built his large house, Moss Park, on the west side of the present Sherbourne Street between Queen and Shuter Streets. Its nearest neighbour was Hazelburn, the home of Samuel Peters Jarvis, in the middle of the present Jarvis Street south of Shuter Street. Both houses were on their owners' country estates, but apparently Moss Park was felt to be a threat to Hazelburn's privacy. In 1828 Mrs. Jarvis wrote to her father, "Mr. Allan's new house...puts us completely in the back ground being three times the size of this and we think Mr. Allan promises himself some amusement in viewing the improvements on Mr. Jarvis premises as he has put twelve windows in the end of the house next to us, which gives it a very odd appearance."[18] In an epidemic of measles, scarlet fever and croup during the winter of 1831-32, eight of Allan's ten children died. Mrs. W. D. Powell wrote, "Allan from a state of indigence is one of the richest men in the community; his house as you know is a Palace; its splendour has become desolation."[19] Moss Park was demolished in 1904.

HOMEWOOD

William Allan gave his surviving son, George William Allan, the land bounded by the present Jarvis, Carlton, Sherbourne, and Bloor Streets. The younger Allan built his house, Homewood, designed by Henry Bowyer Lane, on the present grounds of the Wellesley Hospital in 1848. After his father's death in 1853 he moved into Moss Park, renting Homewood, and finally selling it to Benjamin Homer Dixon ten years later. In 1900 it was bought by Frederic Nicholls, President of the Canadian General Electric Company. It was acquired about 1910 by Dr. Herbert A. Bruce, who turned it into a private hospital, formally opened by Sir Wilfrid Laurier in 1911. The Wellesley Hospital became a public hospital in 1942; over the years there were many large modern additions, and in 1964 the old house was demolished.

HENRY BOWYER LANE
Homewood, 1847
watercolour over pencil
26.4 x 36.6 cm.
AO Horwood Collection

UNKNOWN ARTIST *St Pauls Yorkville*, July 1848 watercolour 17 x 23.8 cm. MTL T10800

ST. PAULS YORKVILLE

Outside the boundaries of the City of Toronto there were a number of smaller communities, usually at important crossroads. Yorkville, north of the present Bloor Street at Yonge Street, was in existence before Toronto was incorporated, and was itself incorporated as a village in 1853, with a population of about eight hundred. It was annexed to Toronto in 1883. Its Anglican parish church, St. Paul's, was built on the Toronto side of Bloor Street between Church and Jarvis Streets. It was designed by John G. Howard and consecrated in 1842. The tower and spire were built horizontally on the ground; it took

six hours to hoist them into position above the little church. The funeral in the foreground of the picture is probably that of a fourteen-month-old boy, because there is a long manuscript poem by the father of the child on the back of the watercolour. It stresses the eternal happiness of Heaven, and ends:

When we think of what our darling is, and what he still must be,
When we muse on that world's perfect bliss and this world's misery,
When we groan beneath this load of sin and feel this grief and pain,
oh we'd rather lose our other two, than have *him* back again.

W. BARTRAM *McGill Cottage*, 185–? oil on board 31 x 37.4 cm. MTL T30581

McGILL COTTAGE

As a former officer in the Queen's Rangers and an important government official, John McGill was granted a hundred-acre park lot between the present Bloor and Queen Streets east of Yonge Street in 1793. He built this house facing Queen Street between Church and Bond Streets shortly afterwards. His heirs lived here in what was called McGill Square until 1870, when the property was sold to the Wesleyan Methodists; it is now occupied by Metropolitan United Church. The unfinished spire of St. Michael's Cathedral can be seen in the background of the painting.

Zion Congregational Church was opened in 1840 on the northeast corner of Bay and Adelaide Streets. It was built of brick covered with plaster made of white marble dust, scored to look like ashlar blocks. In this drawing the Congregational Academy, the Fire Hall and the United Presbyterian Church can be seen north on Bay Street. Zion Church burned down on February 26, 1855. Shortly after, Maclear & Co. published a lithograph drawn by H. Martin that is almost identical to this drawing except for the addition of figures. This watercolour, which probably came from Zion Church, is apparently the original on which the lithograph was based, although it could also be a contemporary copy of the print.

INSANE ASYLUM, TORONTO, CANADA WEST

In the early years of Upper Canada the mentally ill received no treatment; those that were violent or indigent were locked up in jail. After 1840 they were kept in a series of buildings that had become outmoded for other purposes, but in 1844 a government competition "to design a Building for the care (not incarceration) of about 500 of the Insane of Upper Canada"[20] was won by John G. Howard. It was the largest non-military building yet built in Canada. The cornerstone was laid in 1846, and the building opened in 1850 on the south side of Queen Street facing the present Ossington Avenue. This drawing of the south facade in course of construction shows Howard's basic design, with a central block for offices and treatment, and wings on each side for the patients' living quarters and dining rooms. A giant watertank in the dome made possible running water and toilets – a rare luxury in Toronto in 1850. In 1848 the building appears well advanced, but without the cornices and pediments that made it look less stark. Money unfortunately ran out before all of Howard's decorative features were added. The building was demolished in 1976.

ATTRIBUTED TO HENRY MARTIN
Zion Congregational Church, 1855?
watercolour
25.4 x 35.7 cm.
United Church Archives

Insane Asylum, Toronto, Canada West.

AUGUST KÖLLNER
Insane Asylum, Toronto, Canada West, August 15, 1848
pen/ink/wash
18.7 x 22.9 cm.
PAC C13428

In conjunction with the Mechanics' Institute annual art exhibition of 1851, a competition was held for the best picture of Toronto in oils or watercolour, minimum length thirty inches (about 76 cm). The City of Toronto offered a prize of £25, with an option to buy the prize winner at a price fixed by the artist. Four pictures were apparently submitted: a watercolour view from the Island by William Armstrong (price £10), a watercolour by Mr. Toulmin (probably one of the actors of that name in Toronto at the time), a view in oils "from the back" by George F. Price, drawing master at the York County Grammar School (price £35), and Dartnell's view from the Island in oils (price £50). The prize was won by G. F. Price, and his picture was bought for £15, "the actual value of the labour and materials."[21] The City subsequently also bought the Armstrong watercolour, which now hangs in City Hall; the present whereabouts of the painting by Price is unknown. In his letter accompanying his painting Price wrote of the difficulty of painting "a *true* representation" of Toronto because "the very nature of the place" made it impossible to produce "a picturesque work of art"[22] without artistic liberties. There was another problem: in 1851 there were many important buildings being planned or under construction, mainly because of the Great Fire of 1849. Civic pride demanded that the city look its best, or even better; there are definite overtones of the celestial city in Dartnell's painting. To be more than up-to-date he painted buildings not yet built: for example, he included St. James' Cathedral, working from the architects' model now in St. James' Archives. In 1852 Dartnell's painting was shown in an exhibition "in aid of the bazaar for the liquidation of the debt due on the Church of St. George the Martyr," held in the Assembly Chamber of the Parliament Buildings. It was offered for sale for the benefit of the bazaar, but there were apparently no buyers because the painting was acquired from the artist's descendants in 1962.

EDWARD TAYLOR DARTNELL
Panoramic View of the City of Toronto, 1851
oil on canvas
88.9 x 172.7 cm.
ROM SS

SIR SANDFORD FLEMING *St. James' Cathedral and King Street*, 1848 lithograph with one buff tint stone
20.3 x 22.9 cm. PAC C2790

ST. JAMES' CATHEDRAL AND KING STREET

The Anglican diocese of Toronto was established in 1839; its first cathedral, designed by Thomas Young, was begun the same year to replace an earlier St. James' destroyed by fire. A visiting English clergyman, the Rev. A.W.H. Rose, deplored the fact that "some one well versed in ecclesiastical architecture" had not been consulted. "Unfortunately, instead of the decorative style which they of the 'dark ages' knew so well how to employ for sacred purposes, and which has been of late years so happily copied in England in many of our new churches, the building as it stands is one with the commonest possible round-headed windows, and but for the ill-proportioned and stumpy attempt at a spire, might answer as well, or, perhaps, better, as regards exterior, for a corn exchange."[23] This cathedral was itself destroyed in the Great Fire of 1849, and was replaced in 1851-53 by the present correctly Gothic building.

A.R.V. CREASE *St. Georges Church Toronto from My dressing room Window*, July 1851 watercolour and pencil 20 x 26.8 cm. MTL JRR T12594

ST. GEORGES CHURCH TORONTO FROM MY DRESSING ROOM WINDOW

Lieutenant Crease of the Royal Engineers, who lived in rooms on the southwest corner of Queen and John Streets, drew several views from his windows. This one is looking up John Street to the Boulton family's house, The Grange, at the head of the street behind the trees. The Church of St. George the Martyr, built in 1844 on land given by D'Arcy Boulton, was designed by Henry Bowyer Lane, who was also the architect of the other two Anglican churches built in the 1840s, Trinity and Holy Trinity. The *British Colonist* described St. George's as "the handsomest structure of its kind in British America – it unites neatness with convenience, and while due regard is paid to proportion and taste, none of the requisites of a place of worship are sacrificed."[24] St. George's burned down in 1955; only the tower now remains. The artist and engineer, William Armstrong, lived in the cottage surrounded by a fence south of the church. The Lord Nelson Inn, on the northwest corner of Queen and John Streets, was typical of the more than three hundred taverns and grog shops in Toronto at the time.

CUMBERLAND AND RIDOUT, ARCHITECTS *St. James' Parochial School and the Mechanics' Institute*, 1851 watercolour 36.2 x 66 cm. AO Horwood Collection

ST. JAMES' PAROCHIAL SCHOOL AND THE MECHANICS' INSTITUTE

St. James' Parochial School, on the southeast corner of Church and Adelaide Streets, was both a Sunday School and a regular day school, reflecting the close relationship in England between elementary education and the Established Church. It could accommodate six hundred children, with one floor for boys, one for girls, and in the basement a Ragged School for those whose parents could not afford to pay for their education. Although by 1847 municipalities were permitted .to substitute education taxes for school fees, it was not until 1850 that fees were abolished in Toronto's public schools, after a struggle that involved closing the schools completely for the school year 1848-49. At the time St. James' School was built in the early 1850s the issue was still being debated hotly. The Protestant Episcopal Divinity School (later Wycliffe College) was founded in St.

James' School in 1877, moving to the University campus five years later. North of the school was the Toronto Mechanics' Institute building, designed by Cumberland and Storm. Founded on Christmas Eve, 1830, the Mechanics' Institute was a major centre of adult education in Toronto for more than fifty years, with lectures, night classes, concerts, exhibitions, and a lending and reference library. The cornerstone of the building was laid in 1854, but in the middle of 1855 when it was almost completed the Institute ran out of money. The building was leased to the government; it was not until 1861 that the Institute moved in. In 1883 the Mechanics' Institute was taken over by the new Toronto Public Library, and on March 6, 1884, on Toronto's fiftieth birthday, the Library opened in this building. It was demolished in 1950.

GEORGE THEODORE BERTHON   *Osgoode Hall seen from the Southwest*, ca 1852   oil on paper mounted on canvas   31.4 x 42.5 cm.
ROM CC Gift of George Timothy Berthon

OSGOODE HALL SEEN FROM THE SOUTH WEST

Painted from a rear window of Upper Canada College, this view looks across the corner of Adelaide and Simcoe Streets to Osgoode Hall. On the right are the chimneys and garden wall of the Bishop buildings, five fashionable row houses built in 1833 for well-to-do bachelors or small families; on the left is Edward Beckett's brass foundry established on the west side of Simcoe Street about 1852. The east wing of Osgoode Hall was built in 1829-32, and the west wing in 1844. The west wing was designed by Henry Bowyer Lane, who also built a screen in front of earlier living quarters between the two wings, and added a dome. The dome and central part were taken down in 1856-7, and were replaced by Cumberland and Storm's new central building.

This is probably the first illustration of a Toronto event in a Toronto newspaper. It was sketched by Armstrong; "the remainder of the sketch and the drawing on wood is by Mr. Bryce Smith." The locomotive was pulled through the streets from Good's Foundry on the east side of Yonge Street north of Queen Street to the railway yards, creating "a little sensation on King Street a short time since." This was at least the eighth engine built at the foundry, all of which had been delivered through the streets. Good's made the first locomotive ever manufactured in Canada, the *Toronto*, which hauled the first passenger train out of the city on May 16, 1853 – to Aurora and back. St. Lawrence Hall, designed by William Thomas, was built in 1850-51 to replace the Market destroyed in the Great Fire of 1849. For more than twenty years it was a major centre of cultural and social life in the city. Singers like Jenny Lind or the Christy Minstrels, orators like Horace Greeley, celebrities like the tiny General Tom Thumb, all appeared at St. Lawrence Hall. Its popularity, however, declined when larger and more modern theatres and concert halls were built; in this century it was used as a dormitory for the unemployed. Its restoration and rehabilitation was one of the City of Toronto's projects for Canada's centennial in 1967.

GOVERNMENT HOUSE & GROUNDS

Government House, the old part of which had been the home of Chief Justice Elmsley, became the lieutenant governor's official residence in 1815; it stood on the southwest corner of King and Simcoe Streets, the present site of Roy Thomson Hall, and was destroyed by fire in 1862. On May 24, 1854, a procession including the police, members of the Corporation, the fire brigade, some provincial cavalry, the national societies, and citizens generally, passed from City Hall through several triumphal arches on King Street to Government House, where a public meeting was chaired by Mayor J. G. Beard. More than five thousand people attended. Because of the Crimean War there was great patriotic enthusiasm, and the meeting ended with cheers for the Queen, the Emperor of the French and the Sultan of Turkey.

WILLIAM ARMSTRONG
The St. Lawrence Hall, Toronto.
Removal of part of a Grand Trunk
Locomotive from Good's Foundry
to the Company's Works, 1855
wood engraving
22.4 x 22.6 cm.
The Daily Colonist, Toronto 7 March 1855   MTL T30102

LUCIUS O'BRIEN
Government House & Grounds, Toronto C.W.
on the Queen's Birth-day, 1854
lithograph by J. Ellis, Toronto
41.9 x 59.2 cm.
MTL JRR T11870

BERDOE A. WILKINSON *Toronto C.W. Near College Avenue*, ca 1852
watercolour 16.8 x 22 cm. Private Collection

TORONTO C.W. NEAR COLLEGE AVENUE

The first Provincial Agricultural Fair was held in Toronto on the grounds of Government House in 1846. For the next five years it was held in various Ontario towns and cities, returning to Toronto in 1852, when the fair opened in September west of College (now University) Avenue, roughly between the present Queen and Dundas Streets. The grounds were divided by a shallow winding ravine; the southern half, where temporary wooden exhibition buildings and tents were erected, was a field, while the northern part was pleasantly wooded. The

refreshment booth, shown here boarded up, stood on the edge of the ravine near College Avenue. Like all the exhibition buildings it was probably inadequate, since on the busiest day an estimated thirty thousand people attended the fair. In the exhibition buildings themselves, "the crowds…got little more than a glimpse of the various articles exhibited as they were borne along half stifled through the narrow passages."[25] The Provincial Fair returned to Toronto six more times, but Toronto did not have a regular annual exhibition until 1879.

SIR EDMUND WALKER HEAD *University of Toronto*, 1858/9   watercolour   23.2 x 34.8 cm.   University College Archives

UNIVERSITY OF TORONTO

Sir Edmund Head, governor general of Canada, took an intense interest in the building of the University of Toronto (now University College) which was designed by Cumberland and Storm in 1856. The Vice-Chancellor of the University, John Langton, wrote, "Cumberland drew a first sketch of a gothic building but the Gov. would not hear of Gothic and recommended Italian, shewing us an example of the style, a palazzo at Sienna which, if he were not Gov. Gen. and had written a book on art, I should have called one of the ugliest buildings I ever saw. However after a week's absence the Gov. came back with a new idea, it was to be Byzantine; and between them they concocted a most hideous elevation. After this the Gov. was absent on a tour for several weeks during which we polished away almost all traces of Byzantine and got a hybrid with some features of Norman, of early English etc. with faint traces of Byzantium and the Italian palazzo, but altogether a not unsightly building and on his return His Excellency approved."[26] Head continued his role as volunteer architectural consultant – at one point Langton wrote, "I thought Cumberland would have thrown the whole thing up that day, he was so annoyed" – but the cornerstone was laid in October 1856, and the building opened three years later.

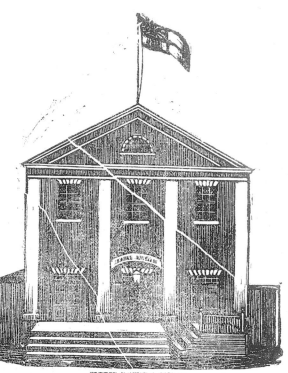

This edifice was built in 1850, and was let to Mr. T. J. Renard in 1851, who opened it with an excellent Stock Company. Mr. Renard left for Australia, and the Toronto Dramatic Association performed there once a week, until Mr. John Nickinson in 1854 took the Lyceum, and after making great internal improvements, opened it with a magnificent Stock company. It was then that the acting of Miss C. Nickinson, and her father, Mr. John Nickinson, displayed itself, and received such laurels for their dramatic achievements.

We have to thank Mr. John Nickinson, for all his trouble and expense in keeping us posted up with the best stars.

THE THEATRE,

In another column will be found a photagraph of Mr. Henry Cooke, a young actor, who since his appearance on the stage has risen so high in the public estimation, that he may ll be called the people's idol.

UNKNOWN ARTIST
Royal Lyceum Theatre, 1858
woodcut by Lyon & Bros.?
12 x 9.5 cm.
The Boy's Times, July 21, 1858
MTL T30671

ROYAL LYCEUM THEATRE

John Ross Robertson, founder of the *Toronto Telegram*, philanthropist and historian, was the editor of the school paper, *The College Times*, when he was a pupil at Upper Canada College. In 1857 he published an issue which upset the school authorities, and his paper was suppressed. The sixteen-year-old Robertson promptly started an unofficial paper called *The Boy's Times*, which he printed himself and sold outside the school gates. The issue of July 21, 1858, contained thirteen illustrations, ten of Toronto buildings (these cuts had appeared in the *Weekly Globe* in 1856), one of Henry Cooke, and two very primitive woodcuts, one of Upper Canada College, and this one of the Royal Lyceum Theatre, printed from a cracked block. Each was accompanied by a brief history and description; this issue was in fact the prototype of Robertson's monumental *Landmarks of Toronto*. The Royal Lyceum, built in 1848 by John Ritchey on the south side of King Street between Bay and York Streets, was leased by T. P. Besnard in partnership with John Nickinson from about 1849 until 1852; from 1853 to 1858 Nickinson was sole proprietor. It was later managed by Mrs. Charlotte Morrison, who as "Miss C. Nickinson" had been admired by the adolescent Robertson. In 1873 the theatre burned down, but Mrs. Morrison went on to open the Grand Opera House, and was a commanding figure in Toronto's theatrical history.

GREAT LIBRARY, OSGOODE HALL

In 1856-7 the central part and dome of Osgoode Hall were demolished, and a larger, more impressive building designed by Cumberland and Storm was begun. The masterpiece of the new building was the Great Library, called by Henry Scadding "noble in its dimensions and aspect,"[27] and by Eric Arthur one of the finest rooms in Canada. Arthur, however, makes two criticisms, both of which are evident in this architect's drawing – "As a reading room, it takes the full glare of the sun and as a library, it was not designed to house books."[28] Additions to Osgoode Hall in the 1880s necessitated the blocking of the window shown here at the east end of the Library.

WILLIAM G. STORM
Great Library, Osgoode Hall, 1856
pen/ink/wash
73.7 x 55.9 cm.
AO Horwood Collection

Part of the present Rosedale area was included in the village of Yorkville. Named from Sheriff W. B. Jarvis' estate, Rosedale was very hilly because two streams meandering through it cut deep ravines. Severn Creek rose near the present corner of Dufferin Street and Eglinton Avenue, and flowed southeast into the Don near the Necropolis, while the smaller Reservoir Creek rose north of Eglinton near Bathurst Street, and joined the Don north of Bloor Street. This watercolour by an unknown Englishwoman is probably of Severn Creek, showing Chief Justice Draper's house, Hazeldean, near the present Collier Street and Park Road.

TORONTO FROM THE DON RIVER

"There is now on exhibition in Mr. Pell's Picture Gallery, a view of Toronto, on a canvas some where about 5 feet by 3 feet by Mrs. Hoppner Meyer. The view is taken from the road in the North Eastern part of the City, leading to the Don and Danforth Road [now Gerrard Street] – and gives an extended range of the City from East to West. In the immediate foreground is the river Don fully brought out to view. The City with its spires and turrets is relieved by the Bay and the Lake in the distance, on which, a steamer and some sailing craft are represented. This is a great work for a lady." The painting thus described in the *Daily Colonist* of June 22, 1855, was offered for sale to the City in April, 1855, and was finally purchased from Mrs. Meyer for £50 in 1857. This view, southwest from roughly the present Broadview and Bain Avenues, shows from left to right Gooderham's windmill, the tower of Trinity Anglican Church, the spire of St. Paul's Roman Catholic Church, and the cupolas of the City Hall and St. Lawrence Hall, with the spires of other churches in the distance. The large building on the right, which looks as though it may have been a later addition to the painting, is the Toronto General Hospital, under construction on the north side of the present Gerrard Street west of Sumach Street. Designed by William Hay, it was begun in 1853 and opened in 1856. It was superceded by the present Toronto General Hospital on College Street in 1913.

UNKNOWN ARTIST
York Town, near Toronto Canada West, 185–?
watercolour
25.4 x 36.2 cm.
Hyla and Walter Fox

MARY HASTINGS (FITZGERALD) MEYER
Toronto from the Don River, 1855
oil on canvas
94 x 160 cm.
Corporation of the City of Toronto

T.H. STEVENSON *The Countess of Elgin & Lady Alice Lambton Receiving the Bouquets & Crest of the College Octr. 20th. 1847 in the Hall of Upper Canada College*, 1848
lithograph printed and published by J. Ellis, Toronto   23.6 x 34.6 cm.   MTL T10263   Gift of Edward F. Nash

THE COUNTESS OF ELGIN & LADY ALICE LAMBTON

At the close of a visit to Upper Canada College by the Governor General, Lord Elgin, flowers were presented to his wife and her sister. Among the College staff sitting on the dais were Henry Scadding (third from left), Principal F. W. Barron (at the lectern), and John G. Howard (on the right). The College janitor, Samuel Alderdice, stood at the extreme right. Howard wrote in his diary on March 9, 1848, "to Mr Ellis's to see Mr Stevenson took a sitting for my likeness in the College group."[29]

By March 22 the *Toronto Examiner* had received this "very beautiful specimen of the Lithographer's Art," and commented that the portraits of Barron and Scadding were particularly accurate. Upper Canada College was built in 1829-30 on land bounded by the present King, Simcoe, Adelaide and John Streets, moving to its present site north of St. Clair Avenue at Avenue Road in 1891. Begun as a school supported by government funds, it became a private school in 1900.

UNKNOWN ARTIST *House of Providence, Toronto, Canada West*, 1855 lithograph with three tint stones par Courtois, imp. Villain, Paris 30 x 51.8 cm. MTL JRR T11957

HOUSE OF PROVIDENCE, TORONTO, CANADA WEST

In 1855, Armand Francis Marie de Charbonnel, second Roman Catholic Bishop of Toronto, announced plans for "a House of Providence in this opulent City" to help "the needy, the immigrants, the old, the invalid, and destitute."[30] It was to be superintended by the Sisters of St. Joseph, who had arrived in Toronto in 1851. Money for the building was raised from a general voluntary collection of a penny a week per person; the Bishop himself gave £500. The House of Providence, designed by William Hay, opened in 1857 on Power Street south of St. Paul's Roman Catholic Church. Its work still continues, since 1962 at Providence Villa and Hospital in Scarborough. The old building was torn down to make way for the Richmond Street ramp to the Don Valley Expressway. Bishop Charbonnel, a native of France, probably arranged for the printing of this lithotint in Paris.

UNKNOWN ARTIST *"The Cottage," Toronto,* 1867 watercolour 12.5 x 17.8 cm. MTL 982-28-14

"THE COTTAGE"

"The Cottage" was one of the first houses designed in Canada by John G. Howard. It was built in 1833 for John Strachan's daughter and her husband, Thomas Mercer Jones, on the northwest corner of the present Front and York Streets, next to Strachan's own large Georgian house. The *Brockville* *Recorder* of October 11, 1833, commented, "Among the buildings in progress intended as the residence of private gentlemen, we may notice that of Mr. Mercer Jones, near the Archdeacon's – the architectural design of which is at once chaste and unique." The house was demolished in 1893.

WILLIAM ARMSTRONG *Arrival of the Prince of Wales at Toronto, September, 1860,* 1860 watercolour 33.7 x 57.8 cm. National Gallery of Canada, Ottawa

ARRIVAL OF THE PRINCE OF WALES

The first official royal visit to Toronto began at sunset on September 7, 1860. The Prince of Wales (later King Edward VII) landed at the foot of John Street, west of the Parliament Buildings, where bleachers surrounded a pavilion and a welcoming arch. The ceremonies opened with the singing of the national anthem by several thousand children. By the time the City's address was presented it was dark and windy; the address was read with considerable difficulty. After the formal welcome, the Prince's carriage was conducted through the brightly illuminated and decorated streets by a great procession of the militia, firemen, and national societies. "Many a year hence," reported the *Globe* next day, "it will be told that on that day the heir-apparent to the British Throne made his public entry into the chief city of the Western Province, and received a welcome surpassing in magnificence and enthusiasm all the public ovations ever before witnessed in the New World."

SIR DANIEL WILSON *Sherbourne Street Blockhouse,* 186–? watercolour 24.3 x 37.6 cm. Private Collection

SHERBOURNE STREET BLOCKHOUSE

In 1838 during the alarms and excursions that followed the Rebellion, several blockhouses were built about a mile from the city. One on Yonge Street near the present Belmont Street, and another at what is now Bloor and Sherbourne Streets remained standing for many years, and were popular subjects for the amateur artist; at least ten paintings and drawings still survive. In these pictures the blockhouses are vaguely domesticated, with the inevitable red cow in the foreground. Thomas Glegg described them in 1841, when they were still of military significance: "They are of 2 stories and made of square logs about 12" thick – A Guard bed is provided for 24 men on the lower Story – trestle bedsteads for 20 men on the Upper – & the usual Barrack fitments. Stoves on the lower floor answer the purposes of warmth & cooking – they are lighted and aired by 3 windows on each story, and loop-holed blocks are ready to fill in the openings when required for defence."[31]

D.C.H. *Presentation of a silver mace to the 2nd Battalion (Queen's Own) Volunteer Rifles, by their Lady Relatives and Friends, 1863* lithograph with touches of red watercolour, drawn and published by the Canada Engraving Establishment, Toronto 23.1 x 49.9 cm. MTL T13231

PRESENTATION OF A SILVER MACE

The Toronto regiment, the Queen's Own Rifles of Canada, was formed in 1860 as the 2nd Battalion Volunteer Militia Rifles of Canada. In 1863 its name was changed to 2nd Battalion or Queen's Own Rifles of Toronto, and on May 25 the regiment was presented with a silver mace made by J. G. Joseph & Co., Toronto, by the wife of Chief Justice William Draper. The ceremony took place on the Normal School grounds (now the Ryerson campus) across from Victoria Street. The Queen's Own Rifles have had a long and impressive history; they first saw active service at the Battle of Ridgeway during the Fenian Raid on the Niagara Peninsula in June, 1866, when seven were killed, two fatally wounded, and twenty others hurt. A monument to the fallen was erected on Queen's Park Crescent west of the present Legislative Buildings in 1870.

Roasin House Toronto. (Morning after fire)

ROSSIN HOUSE, TORONTO (MORNING AFTER FIRE)

Two brothers, Marcus and Samuel Rossin, came from Germany in the 1840s; they began in Toronto as jewellers, but became successful entrepreneurs in other fields as well. In 1857 they opened their hotel, the Rossin House, on the southeast corner of King and York Streets. It was by far the largest and most luxurious hotel in Toronto at the time, and was designed by the Rochester firm of Kauffmann and Bissell (William Kauffmann moved to Toronto in 1856). Its ground floor was built of cast iron with large plate-glass shop windows; above were four storeys of brick with internal brick walls providing structural stability. It could accommodate five hundred guests, at a rate of $2.50 a day. On November 14, 1862, about 2:30 in the morning, a fire started near the kitchen. While the fire brigade fought the blaze with three fire engines, soldiers from the New Fort carried out goods from the ground floor shops and helped the police keep order. One man died; property loss was estimated at two hundred thousand dollars. The two buildings shown here south of the hotel on York Street, the Club Chambers and the Toronto Club, were saved. Although the Rossins themselves left Toronto after the fire, the hotel was rebuilt as the Rossin House, renamed the Prince George Hotel in 1909, and demolished in 1969.

W. S. HATTON
Rossin House, Toronto (Morning after fire), 1863
watercolour on blue-green paper
26.2 x 37.2 cm.
MTL T13287

INDIAN ROAD

By Confederation Toronto was a thriving city, with a population of about fifty thousand. Outside the limits of this city, but well within the boundaries of ours, lay a number of villages and hamlets, farmland, and bush. Indian Road was a long way outside the Toronto of 1867. It was laid out by John G. Howard following an old Indian trail near his property, now High Park. John Ellis was familiar with the area; the Ellis family lived immediately west of Howard on the other side of Grenadier Pond. His sketch looks north on Indian Road, north of the present Garden Avenue.

TORONTO ROLLING MILLS

The coming of the railways in the 1850s had a profound influence on Toronto. For the individual the railways vastly increased the speed and ease of travel; for the merchant they opened up rich new markets and afforded much better access to former suppliers and markets; for the capitalist they provided a lucrative field for speculation; for the industrialist they offered new and greater opportunities. In 1857 the Toronto Rolling Mills Company was founded by a group led by the railway contractor Sir Casimir Gzowski, to re-roll worn rails and to make new wrought iron rails. It was the largest manufacturing industry in Toronto, and the largest iron mills in Canada. When steel rails from England replaced the iron ones, it went out of business, and the plant on the south side of Mill Street between Cherry and Water Streets was closed in 1873.

JOHN ELLIS
Indian Road, 1865
pen & ink
12.7 x 12.7 cm.
MTL T12586
Gift of Mrs. Stone

WILLIAM ARMSTRONG
Toronto Rolling Mills, 1864
pastel
73.2 x 103.2 cm.
MTL JRR T10914

PAUL KANE *Bloor's Brewery, Rosedale Ravine, Toronto,* n.d. watercolour 13.3 x 22.5 cm. ROM DE Gift of Raymond A. Willis

BLOOR'S BREWERY, ROSEDALE RAVINE, TORONTO

Joseph Bloor arrived in York shortly after the War of 1812, and kept an inn called the Farmers' Arms on King Street across from the Market. In the early 1830s he built his brewery on Severn Creek north of the present Bloor Street between the Huntley and Sherbourne Street bridges. The creek was dammed for water power, creating Bloor's Pond, which in the spring sometimes spread almost to Yonge Street. Bloor was active in the subdivision and sale of land in Yorkville, and in 1843 he sold the brewery to John Rose, who called it the Castle Frank Brewery, and operated it until 1864. The building was demolished about 1875. The Sherbourne Street blockhouse stood on rising ground behind the brewery.

D.C. GROSE *View of Toronto*, May 1863 oil on canvas 30 x 40 cm.
AEAC Purchase, Chancellor Richardson Memorial and Wintario matching funds, 1980

VIEW OF TORONTO

This view, looking up the Don River from south of the present Gerrard Street, shows from left to right, the petroleum refinery of Parsons Brothers, the narrow Gerrard Street bridge crossing the river at an angle, and the Don Jail in course of construction. The Ontario petroleum industry began with the opening of North America's first successful oil well in Lambton County by 1858. It boomed during the American Civil War, but the development of the Pennsylvania oil fields after 1865 greatly diminished its profits. At this time oil was used mainly for lamps and for lubricating machinery. Work on Toronto's fourth jail, designed by William Thomas, began in 1858, but a fire in 1862 during its construction postponed its opening until 1865. The tall ventilators rising above each wing were for many years a distinctive feature of the jail.

QUEEN CITY OF THE WEST/1868-1899

CHAPTER TWO

Fair Toronto! Queen City of the West!
Of all thy sister-cities thou art best:
As far as eye can reach, from Don to Humber,
Are chimneys, tow'rs, and spires in goodly number,–
Cathedrals, churches, schools, and mansions rise,
In stately grandeur tow'ring to the skies.

. . .

Long live Toronto! loud her praises swell,
Here Commerce, Art, and Nature love to dwell.[32]

John Imrie was not much of a poet, but when he wrote of his city in the 1880s he was expressing the thoughts of most of the people of Toronto. An endearingly naive boosterism developed in the 1880s and '90s, as its citizens contemplated what God – and man – had wrought in their city. Toronto was booming; its commercial and industrial growth was exceeded only by Brooklyn's in the whole continent. Many books were written extolling the city's past achievements and present glories. Vivid chromolithographs were published of the new buildings – the churches, factories, warehouses and office buildings – and of bird's eye views showing the city's great extent and phenomenal growth. The two most popular symbols of progress were the belching chimney and the telegraph pole, neither now admired. Amateur artists also recorded Toronto, although the *Canadian Illustrated News* of 15 May, 1880, stigmatized their efforts generally as "blottesque if they are bold, skinny if cautious, false in any case."

Even the professional artists were not immune from the prevailing chauvinism. In 1879 when Robert Harris returned to Canada after studying in Paris, he wrote to Lucius O'Brien, one of Toronto's most prominent artists, about the possibility of moving to the city. O'Brien proudly replied, "Toronto is the best art centre in Canada, at present, and there are more artists here than anywhere else, and no lack of portrait painters or rather colourers of photographs....Of book illustrating there is not much at present. Professional models are scarce here, but you can easily get subjects for most things, and in all these facilities we are improving....This, and the country around it, are growing fast and promise to have a great future."[33]

Harris did come to Toronto, arriving on a rainy day in December, 1879. In his letters home to Charlottetown he wrote feelingly of the problems of clients who wanted their portraits to look like photographs, of teaching art to the young ladies at what is now Bishop Strachan School – "I look forward to my next visit with a good deal of horror" – and of using street urchins as models. He commented, "You never saw such a churchgoing town as Toronto, the whole population seems to pour right out of their houses on Sunday. There are an awful lot of churches and they all seem to be full." In another letter he wrote, "There is some fine brick architecture, a great deal of yellow brick is used. St. James Cathedral is a fine place but much spoilt inside by horrid galleries....I got a sketch of a very pretty girl in the Cathedral during the sermon, rather to the distress of an old lady who fixed an eagle eye on my book."[34]

Although Harris himself was only in Toronto for little more than a year, there were a growing number of professional artists in the city. Many of them painted at least a few pictures of Toronto, even if the lure of the Rockies and the Maritimes was very attractive. They dominated the Ontario Society of Artists, founded in 1872, and were prominent in the Royal Canadian Academy of Arts, founded in 1880 with Lucius O'Brien as its first president. In the 1880s and '90s, art, like the city itself, was flourishing.

Despite an international depression, both commerce and industry were expanding enormously. Businessmen from other parts of the province moved to Toronto: men such as the merchant Timothy Eaton from St. Mary's, the manufacturer Hart Massey from Newcastle, and the financier George Cox from Peterborough. In the retail trade, the department stores were introducing a new approach to merchandising. Large factories were replacing the little workshops of artisans. New banks, trust and insurance companies were founded. In 1899 R. G. Dun listed six Toronto firms with assets of more than a million dollars.

The appearance of the city was also changing. "Nothing illustrates the growing opulence of the city more than the character of the places of business and the architectural improvements on the private residences. A shop is not a shop now unless provided with the metropolitan plate glass front, and the tendency in every business is in the shape of extension – in short, to occupy two or three buildings where formerly one was sufficient.... The old square house which was the palace of a merchant years ago, has given place to a building of Elizabethan or other fashionable style, in which the taste for ornamentation is fully gratified."[35]

By 1901 there were 208,040 people living in Toronto, four times as many as there had been in 1867. Although still overwhelmingly British, there were now significant numbers of Germans, Jews, French and Italians. Not all the population growth, however, came from newcomers and natural increase. Between 1883 and 1889 the City annexed more than five thousand acres, increasing its size by more than a half. Much of this land was undeveloped; in 1898 C. S. Clark called it goose pastures, and complained that Toronto "had acquired enough territory to hold all the citizens we are likely to have for the next fifty years."[36]

Most of the city's residents, however, were more optimistic. Besides glorying in the past and present of the city, they had abiding faith in Toronto's future. "It may possibly be a partial pen that indites the sentence, but it certainly seems that, viewed from any and every standpoint, PROGRESS is the indelible handwriting on the walls of Canada's rightly-named 'Queen City.' "[37]

In the 1850s there were a number of paintings and prints depicting the whole city, but during the next decade they were rarely if ever attempted. When such pictures became popular again in the 1870s, they strikingly demonstrate both the growth of the city in the intervening twenty-odd years, as well as the way in which the railways had taken over Toronto's waterfront. In this view northeast from the lake west of the present Spadina Avenue, the Northern Railway wharf and grain elevator are in the foreground with the railway's roundhouse on the Esplanade at the foot of the wharf. In front of St. James' Cathedral can be seen the three towers of the second Union Station; when it was built in 1871-73, it was the biggest, most ambitious railway station in Canada. An engraving after this print by the Photo Engraving Company of New York was frequently reproduced, and was used as the masthead of the *Toronto Advertiser*, beginning January 26, 1878.

G. GASCARD
City of Toronto from the Northern Grain Elevator, ca 1876
lithograph printed with two tint stones by
Alexander Craig, Toronto
36 x 72.2 cm.
MTL JRR T10279

UNKNOWN ARTIST *Immigration Depot, Toronto, 1877* lithograph coloured with watercolour, printed by Maclure & Macdonald, London 6 x 9.8 cm Vignette in *Map of Part of the Province of Ontario for Emigration Purposes*, London, 1877 MTL T30669

IMMIGRATION DEPOT, TORONTO

In 1877 the Province of Ontario published for distribution in England a large sheet extolling the advantages of emigration to the province. The appeal was basically to farmers, with the great inducement that here they would receive free land. On the back of the text was a map of Ontario surrounded by twenty-four coloured vignettes of Ontario scenes, among them five of Toronto showing St. James' and St. Michael's Cathedrals, the Bank of British North America, "Emigrants leaving Union Station for the country," and this one of the Immigration Depot. The Depot was on the Grand Trunk line to Guelph and Sarnia, just north of Fort York. Besides official help and advice, it offered beds and meals "at the lowest prices." It was suggested that "women and children, and small articles of luggage" should be "deposited" at the Depot, and that runners from hotels and taverns be avoided. From the beginning Toronto was the gateway to southwestern and northern Ontario; each year thousands of immigrants passed through the city on their way to its rich hinterland.

JARVIS STREET BAPTIST CHURCH

In Britain both the Baptists and the Methodists were chapel folk. Both began in Toronto with simple meeting houses; by the 1850s the mother churches of each were neo-classical temples. With the building of Metropolitan Methodist Church in 1870, the Methodists broke completely from the chapel tradition, followed by the Baptists in 1875 with Jarvis Street Baptist Church. Designed by Edmund Burke, it was one of the first churches in Canada to use a U-shaped galleried auditorium. Associated with the church were Senator William McMaster, who paid more than half the cost of the new church; A. S. Vogt, organist and choirmaster from 1888 to 1906, who drew most of the singers from the church when he founded the Mendelssohn Choir in 1894; and Dr. T. T. Shields, pastor from 1910 to 1955. Shields often engaged in vehement controversy and seized upon the latest inventions to spread the church's message beyond the pews. In 1922, for example, the "Gospel Car," an open truck covered with texts, drove through the city, while the services were broadcast from the early days of radio.

UNKNOWN ARTIST
Jarvis Street Baptist Church, ca 1875
lithograph by Woodward, Grant & Co., Toronto
47.9 x 36 cm.
Jarvis Street Baptist Church

Taddle Creek was one of the most famous streams that ran through the early city to the lake. It rose somewhere beyond the present Wychwood Park, flowed through the Annex and the University grounds, angled southeastward across the city, and entered the bay at the foot of Parliament Street. A dam near the road that now enters the campus from Queen's Park Crescent created McCaul's Pond, stretching north to the present site of Wycliffe College. Named after Dr. John McCaul, first president of the University, it was described by Professor W.J. Loudon as "a beautiful pond, closed in with forest trees, the eastern edge blue with some curious water flowers; and at the upper end of the still blue surface, a number of wild ducks were swimming about."[38] Taddle Creek and McCaul's Pond added an idyllic note to the University setting, but unhappily they became polluted. *The Varsity* of November 4, 1881, complained, "The stench arising from the Taddle is very pronounced." In 1884 McCaul's Pond was drained and the Taddle buried in a sewer. The artist is looking southwest towards University College across the upper end of McCaul's Pond. It is one of the few paintings of Toronto showing autumn colours.

THE JACKES RESIDENCE, "THE ELMS"

In 1874 Joseph Jackes wrote to his brother, "My home is a large red brick house at the top of a hill, vulgarly known as Gallows Hill, on the right hand side going north. I bought it cheap and have improved it greatly, so that now, with the improvements and the increase in property, it has become worth about $20,000." "The Elms," on the east side of Yonge Street north of Jackes Avenue, was bought by Jackes in 1865 from the family of Walter Rose, who had called it Rose Hill. At that time it was still in the country and had seven acres of grounds, so that, as Jackes reported, "the children are delighted at having plenty of room to play."[39] The Jackes family lived at "The Elms" until 1937; after being used as the office of a used car lot, it was finally demolished about 1948.

LUCIUS O'BRIEN
University College, 1876
watercolour
26 x 36.7 cm.
University of Toronto Archives

UNKNOWN ARTIST
The Jackes Residence, "The Elms," ca 1875
oil on canvas
61 x 81.3 cm.
AGO

ARTHUR COX *Toronto from Bathurst Street Hill*, 1875 oil on canvas 38.1 x 65.7 cm. Private Collection

TORONTO FROM BATHURST STREET HILL

This view, from a promontory in the present Wychwood Park, looks southeast towards the city across Howland Plains, which stretched from Davenport Road to Bloor Street east of Bathurst Street and were used for army manoeuvres. Bathurst Street ended at Davenport Road, where there was a toll gate. In 1875 the tolls, collected by the County of York, ranged from ten cents for each loaded vehicle drawn by two horses or other beasts, to one cent for each sheep, pig, or goat. Most of the toll gates were on the main thoroughfares into the city – Yonge and Dundas Streets and Kingston Road – but supplementary gates like this one were set up to catch travellers using alternative routes to avoid paying toll. In 1896 the tolls were abolished. On the left of the picture is the private carriage drive from Davenport Road up the hill to Davenport, the home of the Wells family. On the right is Seaton Village, developing around Bathurst Street north of Bloor Street.

FREDERICK A. VERNER *Lakeshore Bridge*, 1879 watercolour and pencil 17.8 x 47.5 cm. MTL T12719

LAKESHORE BRIDGE

While the lower reaches of the Don River had been an integral part of the city from the beginning, Toronto's other river, the Humber, was originally almost four miles from the city, and became its western boundary below Bloor Street only in 1967. The Lakeshore Bridge across the Humber at its mouth was built in 1874, south of the Great Western Railway bridge. Its building stimulated the growth of a group of hotels, restaurants, taverns, and boathouses, mostly on the Etobicoke side of the river. Shown here are Charles Nurse's Hotel and Octavius L. Hicks' boathouse; behind Nurse's Hotel was John Duck's Hotel with a wharf that can be seen on the extreme left. Duck, Nurse, and Hicks jointly operated an excursion steamer, the *Ailsa Craig*, which made four trips a day from the city, beginning on the 24th of May each year.

PAUL PEEL   *The Royal Canadian Yacht Club, Toronto Island, 188–?*   oil on canvas   19.7 x 30.5 cm.   Private Collection

THE ROYAL CANADIAN YACHT CLUB

The Canadian Yacht Club was founded in 1852, and was given the right to be called Royal in 1854. Its first clubhouse was an old scow moored near the foot of Simcoe Street, but because of heavy weather and the activities of muskrats it became a wreck. In 1860 the club bought a dismantled freight paddle-steamer, the *Provincial*, and moored it at the same place. The *Provincial* broke from its moorings in the winter of 1869, was frozen in the Bay, and was later blown up by the City. A simple clubhouse was then built near its anchorage. In 1880 the club leased ten acres of marshland on Centre Island, filled and reclaimed it, and built the clubhouse shown here, with its tall tower for watching events in the harbour. Destroyed by fire in 1904, it was replaced in 1906. The new clubhouse burned down in 1918, but was rebuilt almost exactly as before and is still in use.

F.M. BELL-SMITH *Hanlan's Reception, Toronto*, 1879 watercolour 31.8 x 52 cm. THB Marine Museum

Edward ("Ned") Hanlan, who lived on Toronto Island, became an international rowing champion in the 1870s, dominating the sport until 1884. He won the championship of Toronto Bay in 1873, of Ontario in 1875, of Canada in 1877, of the United States in 1878, of England in 1879, and of the world in 1880. After each major victory he was given a tumultuous reception in Toronto. This painting shows his return after winning the English championship. He stands on the pilot house roof of the *Chicora* as it passes the Union Station, surrounded by hundreds of boats of all sizes, many of which had accompanied the *Chicora* all the way from Lewiston, New York. There were crowds on land too; they were so dense in front of the Queen's Hotel that the heavy iron pillar of a letterbox was broken. Toronto's great savant, Goldwin Smith, found offensive "the suggestion that Canada is indebted to a professional oarsman for redemption from obscurity and contempt,"[40] but in his time Ned Hanlan was certainly Canada's most famous citizen.

KING STREET WEST

In 1877 two enterprising brothers from Chicago, Howard and Reuben Belden, arrived in Toronto and began, under several imprints, to publish historical county atlases. At this time there was a vogue for heavily illustrated books, usually issued in parts on subscription, describing a country or continent. The Belden brothers set up a new firm, the Art Publishing Company, in 1880 to publish *Picturesque Canada*. Despite its American origins, the work was intended to be thoroughly Canadian; the art director was Lucius O'Brien, president of the Royal Canadian Academy, and the editor was Principal G. M. Grant of Queen's University. Amid bitter squabbling the idea that the book be a grand showcase for Canadian artists was not realized; of the roughly 543 illustrations in *Picturesque Canada*, 452 were drawn by Americans. Well over two hundred of these were by Schell, called by art historian Dennis Reid "quite frankly a hack."[41] This drawing of King Street looking west from east of Bay Street, shows on the north side, from right to left, the Canada Life Assurance Company Building, the Cawthra house, and, across Bay Street, the Mail Printing House. The view with its broad street and almost Flemish feeling is unlike the wood engraving in *Picturesque Canada*, which is very close to photographs of the same place and time.

VIEW ON KING STREET

This etching, shown at the first annual exhibition of the Association of Canadian Etchers in 1885, shows King Street east of Church Street, with St. James' Cathedral, St. Lawrence Hall, and a horse-drawn streetcar. The first streetcar tracks were laid in 1861 on Yonge Street from King Street to the Yorkville Town Hall, on King Street from Yonge to St. Lawrence Hall, and on Queen Street from Yonge to the Lunatic Asylum. By 1884 there were thirty miles of track giving service on ten lines. Although an electric street railway line had been installed in the Exhibition grounds in 1883, the first electrified cars did not appear on Toronto streets until 1892, and the last horse-car was withdrawn from service in 1894.

FRED B. SCHELL
King Street West, ca 1882
watercolour, gouache over pencil on board
22.5 x 22.6 cm.
Corporation of the City of Toronto

W. J. THOMSON
View on King Street, 1885
etching with surface tone on Japanese paper
18.9 x 18.1 cm.
MTL T12639   Bequest of J. Ross Robertson

F. M. BELL-SMITH *Lights of a City Street*, 1884   oil on canvas   132.7 x 200 cm.   Simpson's Limited

LIGHTS OF A CITY STREET

This busy scene is at the corner of King and Yonge Streets, the hub of Toronto in the last decades of the nineteenth century. The man lifting his hat is the artist's son, while the artist himself is shown buying a newspaper. At this time there were five daily newspapers in Toronto, sold on the streets by swarms of newsboys. In 1898 (after the *Star* was founded and the *Mail* acquired the *Empire*) C. S. Clark wrote, "The great stand for the boys is on the corner of Yonge and King streets, and at the railway stations, where in the mornings you hear the cry 'Globe, Mail & Empire, World,' while in the evening, 'Globe, Mail & Empire, News, Telegram and Star' is rattled off as [fast as] their tongues can utter them. Some little fellows, however, of limited capital confine themselves to the Telegram, and at six o'clock

the streets are full of little shavers yelling 'six o'clock Telegram.' At the time of the Whitechapel horrors [murders by Jack the Ripper], it was a rare harvest for them, and sometimes when there was no Whitechapel murders on the boards, they called it out anyway. These lads are as a rule bright, intelligent little fellows, who would make good and useful men if they got a chance, but some of them are simply stupid. Some of them have no shoes, no coats and even their shirts are merely apologies for such, and yet they are rarely if ever sick...but the cold must necessarily tell upon them in time....A good many of the regular newsboys sell the newspapers in the early morning and black boots part of the day, taking up the newspapers again in the evening. Their ages run from ten to sixteen years."[42]

ROBERT HARRIS *The Family of J. T. M. Burnside of Toronto*, 1880   oil on canvas   86.4 x 99.1 cm.   Mr. and Mrs. Fred Schaeffer

THE FAMILY OF J. T. M. BURNSIDE OF TORONTO

These typical Victorian children were painted by Harris shortly after he arrived in Toronto. They came to his studio every morning; Harris described painting them in his letters home to Charlottetown. "Dot, the eldest girl, is nine, old enough to keep quiet, and we keep up a constant talk. The next, the boy, is about six. I have to tell stories to him without a moment's hesitation for the whole morning, as it is the only way to keep him in his chair. There he sits, with eyes ready to pop out of his head while I tell fearsome tales of dragons or of fairies. Sometimes he is so taken up that he keeps his position till all his limbs go to sleep. The next child I am getting in the act of winding a top, and he has been induced to perform so often that now he regards that plaything in the same light as a dose of medicine. Norah, the baby, is just big enough to meander round the room and to fight like a wildcat when they try to hold her in a position. I want to have this picture ready for the exhibition here. The size is four by four feet, *and it will be a picture, quite irrespective of the portraits*. I mean that, though they are portraits, it won't depend for its content on that only."[43] J. T. M. Burnside was an inspector with the Bank of Toronto, living on St. Vincent Street.

NORWAY HOUSE, EAST TORONTO

In 1834 the Norway Steam Sawmills were established near the corner of Woodbine Avenue and Kingston Road by the Montreal ironmongers, Wragg & Co., which advertised Norway pine as a specialty. An unincorporated village called Norway developed around the crossroads and the mill, including stores, taverns, hotels, and an Anglican Church, St. John's Norway. Ira Bates of Scarborough bought the hotel, Norway House, about 1870, and managed it for almost thirty years. Standing on the south side of Kingston Road just east of Woodbine Avenue, it was typical of many hotels in the suburbs of Toronto, heavily patronized by farmers on their way to and from market. Converted to other uses, Norway House was damaged by fire and finally torn down in the 1960s. East Toronto was incorporated as a village in 1888, proclaimed a town in 1903, and annexed by the City of Toronto in 1908. The artist was Mayor of East Toronto in 1907.

YONGE STREET WHARF

Throughout the nineteenth century travel by water remained popular, and wharves were crowded with passengers and their luggage. The paddle steamer *Algerian*, 456 tons, shown here on the west side of the Yonge Street Wharf, began running between Toronto and Montreal in 1875 for the Richelieu and Ontario Navigation Company, later the Canada Steamship Lines. In 1880 Walt Whitman travelled from Toronto to Kingston by boat. "I write this in Toronto, aboard the steamboat, the *Algerian*, 2 o'clock p.m. We are off presently. The boat from Lewiston, New York, has just come in – the usual hurry with passengers and freight – and as I write, I hear the pilot's bells, the thud of hawsers unloosened, and feel the boat squirming slowly from her ties, out into freedom." He described the *Algerian*, which arrived in Kingston at sunrise the following day, as "middling good-sized and comfortable carrying shore-freight and summer passengers."[44] The boys in the foreground hold a cricket bat and a lacrosse stick, equipment for Victorian Canada's two most popular summer games.

J. McPHERSON ROSS
Norway House, East Toronto, 1886
oil on canvas
29.6 x 39.9 cm.
Private Collection

F. M. BELL-SMITH
Yonge Street Wharf, 1887?
grey & black wash with
touches of white gouache
18.4 x 28.9 cm.
MTL JRR T10931

JOHN C. FITCH HOUSE

This house, which stood on the west side of Jarvis Street north of Isabella Street, is typical of the many large houses built in the 1880s on Jarvis Street, then one of the most fashionable streets in the city. Fitch had been a wholesale grocer and commission merchant in partnership with Sir William P. Howland. In the 1870s he was involved with the Toronto and Nipissing Railway Company, and was the first president of the Standard Bank of Canada. He moved into his big house at a time of personal tragedy – his son, Lieutenant W. C. Fitch of the Royal Grenadiers, was killed at the Battle of Batoche in May, 1885. More than six hundred men in Toronto's militia regiments made the long journey to the West in the campaign that finally defeated Louis Riel and his followers at Batoche.

BARBARA AND ALICE, QUEEN'S PARK

In the 1880s Queen's Park was by far the most popular park in Toronto. With the spacious university grounds across Taddle Creek on the west, there were almost a hundred acres of trees and meadow – a favourite resort especially in the hot weather. Band concerts were held in the Park, and anyone with a soapbox could hold forth at the speakers' corner, but this was later prohibited because too many people were using their fists as well as their tongues. G. Mercer Adam called the building of the present Legislative Buildings "a questionable intrusion on the recreation grounds of the people."[45] Barbara and Alice were the artist's daughters; this painting may have originally been called "Happy Days," and have been shown at the Ontario Society of Artists exhibition in 1886.

WILLIAM G. STORM
House of John C. Fitch, 1884
watercolour
34.9 x 49.3 cm.
AO Horwood Collection

MARMADUKE MATTHEWS
Barbara and Alice, Queen's Park, 1886
oil on canvas
63.5 x 76.2 cm.
AGO
Gift of Trinity College, University of Toronto, 1967

J. SHORT McMASTER.
LONDON, ENG.

HENRY W. DARLING.
TORONTO.

Mc MASTER, DARLING & CO.

ESTABLISHED 1844.

McMASTER DARLING & CO.

WHOLESALE DRY GOODS IMPORTERS.　　　TORONTO · CANADA.

UNKNOWN ARTIST *McMaster, Darling & Co.*, 1886? chromolithograph by Rolph, Smith & Co., Toronto
54.3 x 75 cm. MTL T12326

McMASTER, DARLING & CO.

By the 1860s, dry goods wholesalers were Toronto's wealthiest merchants. William McMaster, who had founded his wholesale dry goods firm in Toronto in 1844, had the largest such concern in Ontario in 1860; he transferred it to his nephews, A. R. McMaster and Brother in 1863, and the firm became McMaster, Darling & Co. about 1886. This warehouse was built in 1871 on Front Street west of Yonge Street, then the centre of the wholesale district. At eighty feet it was much taller than earlier commercial buildings, because its elevator – an innovation in Toronto in the 1870s – made its four storeys with high ceilings practical. Although it was designed in the fashionable Second Empire style criticized by fire underwriters because of the lofty mansard roofs and wooden dormers, the building served a valuable purpose during the Great Fire of 1904, when almost

twenty acres of downtown Toronto were devastated. Shortly before nine o'clock on a cold, blustery evening in April, fire broke out in a necktie factory on Wellington Street west of Bay Street. Strong winds carried the flames southeast, until the fire reached the McMaster building, then an underwear factory, about three o'clock in the morning of April 20. Here the exhausted firemen made a stand; the old warehouse was damaged but not destroyed, and the fire spread no further east. Rebuilt and enlarged after the fire, the McMaster building was finally demolished in 1960. The Bank of Montreal, designed by Darling and Curry, and built in 1885 on the northwest corner of Yonge and Front Streets, can be seen on the right. As was the custom, the manager lived above the bank; his apartment with its handsome fireplaces and mouldings is now used for storage.

UNKNOWN ARTIST *Confederation Life Building*, 1890 chromolithograph 71.2 x 107.7 cm. D. S. Richardson

CONFEDERATION LIFE BUILDING

In 1890 four major Toronto office buildings were under construction, for the Board of Trade, the Canadian Bank of Commerce, the Canada Life Assurance Company and the Confederation Life Association. All were designed by architects who had been practising in the United States, where their style had been strongly influenced. All four rose high above the earlier commercial buildings, with six or seven storeys to their three or four. They represented Toronto's financial hegemony over the rest of the province and the newly opening West. (Canada Life's head office was still in Hamilton, but it moved to Toronto in 1899.) Of the four, only the Confederation Life Building, designed by Knox and Elliot, formerly of Chicago, with Beaumont Jarvis of Toronto, is still standing, on the northeast corner of Yonge and Richmond Streets. The Confederation Life Association was founded in 1871 with Sir Francis Hincks as president, and Senator William McMaster as vice president; Sir William P. Howland became president in 1874. Hincks and Howland had both served as Canadian ministers of finance, while McMaster was president of the Canadian Bank of Commerce, so that the new company had strong ties with both government and finance. By 1885 it was the second largest Canadian life insurance company, surpassed only by Canada Life.

When the first steamboat sailed into Toronto harbour in 1817 a prominent merchant, John Spread Baldwin, wrote, "She will ruin all the Shipping on the Lake make 3 voyages to their one, but it is a very expensive concern & tis thought will not make any thing for her owners."[46] By mid-century sailing vessels were no longer used for passenger service, but they still transported bulk freight, because although slower they were cheaper than the steamboats. This view shows the wharves at the foot of Yonge Street, and the Great Western Railway Station on the left. Designed by William G. Storm, it was built in 1866 on the northeast corner of Yonge and Esplanade Streets. Later used as a produce market, it burned down in 1952.

JOHN COLIN FORBES
Toronto Bay, ca 1874
oil on canvas
53.3 x 98.4 cm.
Private Collection

CLARENCE SQUARE

Toronto

FROM NORTH SIDE

ROBERT J. WYLIE, JR. *Clarence Square from the North Side*, 1886 watercolour and gouache over pencil 31.6 x 49.5 cm. ROM SS

The area northeast of Fort York was originally reserved for military purposes. In the 1830s part of it was transferred to the civil government, and in 1837, by order of the Lieutenant Governor, Sir Francis Bond Head, a plan was drawn for its subdivision into city blocks. On this plan Clarence Square was joined to Victoria Square, which lay further west between Portland and Bathurst Streets, by a broad tree-lined drive named Wellington Place, later Wellington Street. Clarence Square was named for the Duke of Clarence, the former title of King William IV; Victoria Square was named for Princess Victoria, the King's heir. Two large houses were built in the early

1870s on the east side of Clarence Square facing Wellington Street; smaller row houses were built on the north and south sides later in the same decade. The Square itself and most of the houses on the north side are all that remain of the amenities planned in 1837 – Wellington Street between Spadina Avenue and Portland Street is certainly no shady promenade, and Victoria Square has completely disappeared, with Wellington Street extending right across it; only the Old Military Burying Ground has not been built upon. Residential squares were never a common feature of Toronto; Clarence Square is one of the very few that survive.

UNKNOWN ARTIST *The Queen's Hotel,* ca 1887 coloured lithograph by Rolph, Smith, & Co., Toronto
50.5 x 60.5 cm. PAC C119990

THE QUEEN'S HOTEL

In 1838 a terrace of four houses was built on the north side of Front Street between Bay and York Streets. Knox College combined the houses and occupied them from 1844 to 1856, when the building became an hotel. In 1862 Captain Thomas Dick became the proprietor, naming it the Queen's Hotel. The Queen's, greatly enlarged over the years, was close to the Parliament Buildings and to the Union Station west of York Street, with a clear view of the lake obstructed only by the Jacques and Hay furniture factory south of its eastern garden. Behind it was H.J. Boulton's Scottish baronial Holland House. "Our specialty was English aristocracy," said Antony Gilchrist, an old employee. "We had nothing but the best families." Among visitors at the Queen's were several members of the British royal family, Grand Duke Alexis of Russia (whose suite occupied an entire floor), Sir Henry Irving, Ellen Terry, Sarah Bernhardt (who created a disturbance in the middle of the night because her room was noisy), Adelina Patti, Jefferson Davis and General Sherman. During parliamentary sessions in Toronto, Sir John A. Macdonald lived in Room 52 with the Red Parlour where many important discussions took place leading to Confederation. Sir George Etienne Cartier, however, stayed in another hotel. "I don't recall any Frenchman at the Queen's," Gilchrist said. "We were rather an English hotel, but I do remember Captain Dick lighting Chinese lanterns in the maple trees in front of the hotel to celebrate confederation."[47] There were always a number of more or less permanent residents at the Queen's, including thirty or forty Southerners during the American Civil War. By the 1920s the great days of the Queen's were coming to an end. In 1927-28 it was demolished to make way for the Royal York Hotel.

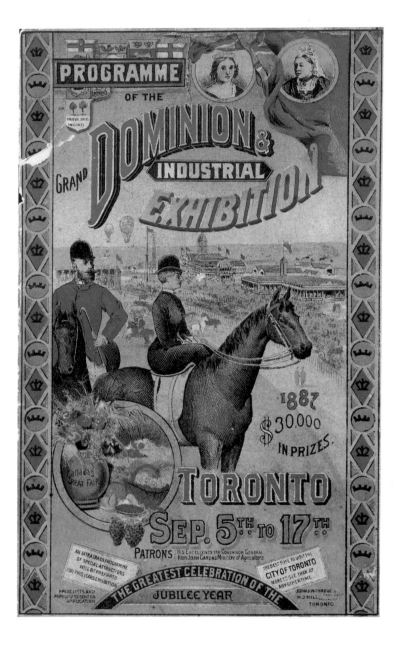

UNKNOWN ARTIST
Programme of Dominion Industrial Exhibition, 1887
chromolithograph by Mail Job Printing Co., Toronto
13.5 x 8 cm.
Canadian National Exhibition Archives

From 1846 the Provincial Agricultural Fair perambulated about Ontario, never in the same city for two consecutive years. This meant that in most cities the buildings and grounds were temporary; as attendance at the fairs grew larger because of improved transportation and increased population and prosperity, more facilities were required. Toronto defeated Guelph and Ottawa in bidding for the 1878 fair. Hoping that the fair would be held permanently in Toronto, the City leased more than fifty acres of the old Garrison Reserve from the Dominion Government (the nucleus of the present Exhibition Park), and spent seventy-five thousand dollars in erecting twenty-five buildings in three months, despite the fact that this expenditure had twice been voted down by the ratepayers. The central building was the Crystal Palace made of cast iron and glass, incorporating a smaller building built for the 1858 Provincial Fair that was moved to the site. When the 1879 Provincial Fair was awarded to Ottawa despite Toronto's great efforts and expense, the Toronto City Council organized a rival Industrial Exhibition Association, which held its first exhibition in Toronto in 1879. Despite its name its emphasis was still agricultural, reflecting the nature of the province, but there were a significant number of exhibits of machinery and inventions, some of them in operation. By 1887 the annual Industrial Exhibition was well established; its name was changed to the Canadian National Exhibition in 1904. During the 1880s there were several innovations at the Exhibition. In 1882 it was the first fairground in the world lit by electricity, in 1883 the first electric streetcar in Canada was installed, and in 1886 the first Labour Day celebrations in Canada were held. In 1887, while the grandstand show was "The Siege of Pekin" complete with fireworks, a popular exhibit was Queen Victoria modelled in wax. Toronto had always been a royalist city, but Queen Victoria's jubilees of 1887 and 1897 were celebrated with particular gusto. It was the heyday of the British Empire and its never-setting sun; Toronto shared in the imperialist euphoria of the late Victorian period.

GEORGE A. REID *Toronto Bay, 1886*, 1887 oil on canvas 54.5 x 137.7 cm. MTL JRR T10363

"Although not a picturesque city, Toronto is not lacking in natural and artistic beauty. Its chief adornment is its water-front, as seen from the harbour and island, or the lake beyond. The approach by water, either by the gap or by the western entrance to the harbour, is singularly fine. The spires, towers and cupolas of its churches and public buildings, with the imposing array of substantial warehouses that line the shore-front, afford an agreeable contrast to the confused mass of the city, sloping up in the distance, and mark it as a place of wealth and enterprise."[48] This painting, which was shown in the Ontario Society of Artists exhibition of 1887, depicts the waterfront from Simcoe to Frederick Streets, with the Union Station on the left and St. Lawrence Hall on the right.

In 1859 the Western Auxiliary School was opened on Givins Street, after three years in rented premises. It was a one-storey frame building with two rooms, one for boys and one for girls, in each of which all grades were taught. The year before, the one teacher, Mrs. O'Flaherty (salary $320 a year), had had eighty-four pupils in ten grades. In the new building (named Givins Street Public School in 1860) at least there were two teachers, but by 1871 there were about 250 pupils enrolled, although the truant officer reported that the lack of sidewalks and the bad state of the roads often kept the smaller children at home. At this time Argyle Street was a cedar swamp, and Dovercourt Road was impassable in the winter and spring, with a deep ditch down the east side to carry off the water. In 1876 the building was sold for $155 to the Wesley Methodist Church, who moved it up Ossington Avenue to use as a Sunday School, and a new school was built with four classrooms. By 1883, "Miss Frozen [i.e. Fraser] has a room seated for 72, a class numbering 107, and an average attendance of about 90....There are about 25 children awaiting admission to this school."[49] More rooms were added, but the number of pupils always exceeded the space available. A larger school was built in 1915, but part of the old school was still used until 1956, when the present school was built, and the former buildings were both demolished.

HEAD OF ST. GEORGE STREET

The Annex, lying between Bloor and Dupont Streets from east of Bedford Road to Kendal Avenue, became part of the city in 1887. At that time only a few houses had been built, mainly around Walmer Road. In the 1890s streets were extended, new streets laid out, and substantial houses, many of them in the romanesque revival style, gave the Annex its distinctive appearance. This view of St. George Street between Dupont Street and Bernard Avenue, looking east, shows the street before houses were built, with the tower of the Church of the Messiah in the distance on Avenue Road.

W. C. HEPBURN
Givins Street Public School, 1895
watercolour
26.7 x 41.3 cm.
Givins Senior Public School   TBE

JOSEPH T. ROLPH
Head of St. George Street, 1890
watercolour
27.6 x 36.4 cm.
MTL JRR T12781

FREDERICK H. BRIGDEN *At Massey Hall*, 189–? pencil 8.5 x 11.8 cm. OHF/MTL T12931

AT MASSEY HALL

In 1892 Hart Massey of the Massey-Harris Company bought land on the southwest corner of Victoria and Shuter Streets and commissioned a Cleveland architect, S.R. Badgley, to design a large music hall as a gift to the citizens of Toronto. The cornerstone was laid by six-year old Vincent Massey. Massey Music Hall (its name was changed to Massey Hall in 1933) opened with a performance of Handel's *Messiah* in May, 1894. Although the *Canadian Architect and Builder* of June, 1894, fumed about "an American architect" and an exterior "about as aesthetical as the average grain elevator," the acoustics of the hall were very highly praised. Besides performances by the world's leading orchestras and soloists, and lectures by people like Bertrand Russell and Winston Churchill, great meetings have been held in Massey Hall where virtually every social and political position has been defended or attacked. The Toronto Art Students' League, founded in 1886, included Brigden, A.H. Howard, C.M. Manly, C.W. Jefferys, T.G. Greene, and J.E.H. MacDonald. Each member was supposed to make at least one sketch each day – one of the League's mottos was "Nulla dies sine linea." This sketch was probably one of Brigden's NDSL drawings.

J.E. USHER *University College Fire*, 1890 oil on canvas 74.5 x 112.5 cm. University College Archives

UNIVERSITY COLLEGE FIRE

On Valentine's Day, 1890, the University College Literary Society was holding a conversazione, while the men in residence in the west wing were having a dance in the dining hall. The College was gaily decorated, and there were displays throughout the building: for example, the Biology Department was exhibiting microscopic examples of the recently discovered "Grippe Microbe." A servant called Pride was carrying a tray of lit coal oil lamps along the front corridor, when he tripped on the few steps down to the southeast door. The lamps ignited the wooden floor, and fire swept the building. Water pressure for the hoses was inadequate; by the time the fire was extinguished most of the east wing of the College was destroyed, including the Library in East Hall with thirty-three thousand books valued at one hundred thousand dollars.

In 1884 Dr. Mulvany wrote that beneath St. Lawrence Hall "is a central arcade, the first half of which, opening on King Street, is occupied by stalls teeming with children's toys, nick-nacks, cheap jewellery, and perfumery, the candies and sweet stuff which Disraeli, in one of his novels, calls 'the opium of childhood,' and second-hand books, which are the opiates of old age! After this comes the butchers' stalls, opening into the arcade, and each of them opening also into the east and west sides of the market square, where are ranged the farmers' carts laden with dairy produce, meat, and vegetables. The show of meat in the market, as also of cheese and butter, is well worth a visit; the writer has seen nothing equal to it in any other Canadian city. But the best time by far to visit St. Lawrence Market is at Christmas or New Year season; then the huge beef-carcases, rich with fat, hang side by side, some of the finest labelled with the name of some hotel proprietor or prominent citizen, who may have purchased that splendid provision for the Christmas feast; there, to use Chaucer's phrase, it seems 'to have snowed of meat and drink;' there the huge deer, 'the fat and greasy citizens' of our forests, are suspended, picturesque with branching antlers; there, too, is the black bear, in plump condition ere winter has thinned his fair porportions – a leading *restaurateur*, Messrs. Clow & Jewell, or Mr. Thomas, has purchased the carcase, and you shall order bearsteak for breakfast – it is more delicate than beef and quite as nutritious. There are big pigs and suckling pigs, such as that of which Charles Lamb wrote so feelingly as a dish to be dealt delicately with, 'deal tenderly with him, he is a weakling, a flower!' There, too, are all manner of birds of the air, the huge wild turkey, sometimes the rare wild swan, the prairie chicken, grouse and partridge, besides all the tribes of Grallatores and Natatores. Brilliantly illuminated, brightly decorated, St. Lawrence Market is undeniably one of the things worthy of being seen in Toronto during the Christmas holidays."[50] In 1951 the National Ballet of Canada began to use parts of St. Lawrence Hall. After the restoration of the Hall in 1967, the market area became the foyer of the Hall and the National Ballet's scenery workshop.

FREDERICK H. BRIGDEN
The Market in Winter, 1898
pen & ink, reproduced in Toronto Art Students'
League *Calendar*, 1899
18 x 14 cm.
MTL

HARRY SPIERS *Street Hawker near St. Lawrence Market*, 1897 watercolour, gouache on paper
50.7 x 40.5 cm. Corporation of the City of Toronto
On permanent loan from Mrs. R.S. Kingsmill

STREET HAWKER NEAR ST. LAWRENCE MARKET

This soapbox salesman is selling a red liquid – patent medicine? – outside a tavern, possibly on the northeast corner of Front and Jarvis Streets. Patent medicines were very popular in the 1890s and were advertised extensively in the newspapers and magazines of the day, with glowing testimonials, often from reverend gentlemen with vague addresses. Legislation controlled the practice of medicine in Ontario, so that Toronto did not have quack doctors, but quack medicines circulated freely, and were openly sold on streetcorners. Most of them did little harm; some of them with narcotic or alcoholic bases might at least give the patient a short relief from pain.

T. MOWER MARTIN *Open Air Service*, 1895 oil on canvas 244 x 365.7 cm. Salvation Army, Canada and Bermuda Territory

OPEN AIR SERVICE

The Salvation Army began work in Toronto in 1882, with its street preaching and its emphasis on the reclamation of the unfortunate. In the beginning its meetings were often disrupted by abuse and violence, and Salvationists were sometimes arrested for refusing to move on when directed by police. As Senior-Major Arnold Brown of the Salvation Army wrote, "In Toronto, open-air fighting was an important part in the interest-arousing efforts of the Salvationists."[51] In 1883 the Richmond Street Barracks was opened, and in 1886 the Toronto Temple and Territorial Headquarters at the northeast corner of Albert and James Streets. In 1886, also, the founder of the Salvation Army, "Your affectionate General" William Booth, paid his first visit to Toronto; the Toronto Temple had the largest religious auditorium in the city, but it was still inadequate for the crowds. Although isolated instances of hooliganism still occurred, the days of oppression for the Army in Toronto were over, because the value of its work had become evident. In this scene at the corner of Queen and Chestnut Streets, roughly in front of the present City Hall, the artist used Salvationists as models for all the figures in the painting, including the semi-recumbent drunk. Several of them were on the *Empress of Ireland* when it sank in the St. Lawrence River in 1914 with 167 Salvationists on board; some of the 150 that were lost are buried in a special plot near the main gates of Mount Pleasant Cemetery.

HARRY SPIERS *Toronto Island*, 1896 watercolour 17.9 x 25.2 cm. Corporation of the City of Toronto

TORONTO ISLAND

Just before Confederation, ownership of Toronto Island was transferred from the Province of Canada to the City of Toronto. The main concern was protection of the harbour; the opening of the Eastern Gap by storms in April 1858 was narrowing the Western Gap. The removal of sand from the Island by builders had also eroded the harbour's natural protection. A program of dredging and building breakwaters was undertaken by the City in conjunction with the new Dominion government. At that time there were several hotels on the Island and a number of fishermen's homes at Hanlan's Point. The City immediately prepared a plan dividing the Island into five-acre lots for lease, and gradually a large summer colony developed. Summer homes ranged from the huge, ornate, frame cottages built by families like the Masseys and the Gooderhams on Centre Island, to a tent town on Ward's Island. At Hanlan's Point near Ned Hanlan's hotel, there was an amusement park, with a merry-go-round, grandstand, and baseball stadium. By the late 1890s the Toronto Ferry Company was operating twelve ferryboats to the Island. In 1900 Baedeker called it "the Margate or Coney Island of Toronto," with all the "paraphernalia of a Cockney paradise."[52] The advantages of such a summer resort so close to the mainland were fully appreciated. As G. Mercer Adam wrote in 1882, "The purposes to which the Island and water-surroundings of Toronto may be put, in affording the means of rest and enjoyment to its jaded citizens, are yet almost undreamed of."[53]

COUNCIL CHAMBER IN OLD CITY HALL

Although its architect, Henry Bowyer Lane, was responsible for several fine buildings in Toronto, the 1844 City Hall on the southwest corner of Front and Jarvis Street was not one of his masterpieces. Dr. Mulvany called it one of the ugliest buildings in the city, while another writer in 1885 went even further, calling it "simply an eyesore, though little more favourable can be said of its surroundings, while its unsanitary condition is a perennial source of discomfort and danger to its occupants."[54] It was replaced by the City Hall at the head of Bay Street in 1899. In 1901 the South St. Lawrence Market was opened, incorporating the old building. After renovations in 1975-77, the Council Chamber, shown here looking north, is now the Market Gallery of the City of Toronto Archives. This mayor's eye view of the Chamber is one of a number of small vignettes in an elaborate testimonial presented to a retiring alderman. Such testimonials were popular from about 1880 to 1920, and often contain charming little exterior and interior views of Toronto buildings.

THE LEGISLATIVE BUILDING

College (now University) Avenue, laid out in 1829, was intended to provide a stately approach to the proposed university, King's College, which was to be built where the Legislative Buildings now stand. Only one university building was erected, which was found to be inadequate. The university, reconstituted as the University of Toronto, moved to the west and built the University College building which opened in 1859. Meanwhile the Avenue served no useful purpose, lying far beyond the actual city. The Legislative Buildings, opened in 1893, were the result of an international competition in 1880, which ended amid much controversy with the choice of a design by one of the judges in the competition, R. A. Waite of Buffalo. Bicycling was extremely popular in the 1890s, both for transportation and recreation; even the future Prime Minister of Ontario, Sir James Pliny Whitney, complete with bowler hat, bicycled each day between his home and the Legislative Buildings. Electric arc lamps were installed on Toronto streets in 1884.

A. H. HOWARD
Council Chamber in Old City Hall, 1894
watercolour
12.9 x 9 cm.
Vignette in "Testimonial to
Alderman Bernard Saunders"
Corporation of the City of Toronto

N. W.
The Legislative Building, seen from University Avenue, 1897
pastel
32.4 x 49.9 cm.
OHF/Government of Ontario

UNKNOWN ARTIST *Cobban Manufacturing Company, Toronto*, ca 1890   chromolithograph by Rolph, Smith & Co., Toronto
52.8 x 73.2 cm.   MTL 982-12

COBBAN MANUFACTURING COMPANY, TORONTO

Founded in 1874, Cobban's employed 125 people by 1885, in the manufacture of mouldings, looking glasses, frames, and all kinds of cabinet work. It imported plate-, German and sheet-glass, making a specialty of plate-glass and silvering. Its factory, two hundred by fifty feet, was on the southeast corner of Teraulay (now Bay) and Hayter Streets. Lieutenant Governor Simcoe had tried to enforce simple zoning regulations when his town of York was planned in 1796; this had not worked then, and was not even considered throughout the nineteenth century, when factories, offices, and houses were indiscriminately intermingled. By the 1890s, however, many factories were relocating near the railway lines because of the great advantage of proximity to transportation; about 1897 Cobban's moved to the lakeshore south of the present Union Station. During the Great Fire of 1904 its president, Francis J. Phillips, and his foreman saved the million feet of lumber in its yards by running from stack to stack with a garden hose and a trickle of water, as huge pieces of burning material blew across the railway tracks. Cobban's former uptown factory stood vacant until after the turn of the century. This print is typical of many views of factories published from the 1880s to the first World War, in which dense black smoke is equated with progress and prosperity.

C.M. MANLY *History and Progress*, 1899 pen & ink, reproduced in Toronto Art Students' League *Calendar*, 1900
11 X 14 cm MTL

HISTORY AND PROGRESS

In the nineteenth century Toronto's interest in its own history was inextricably interwoven with the Victorian belief in the inevitability of progress. During the semi-centennial celebrations of 1884, "one is unconsciously taken back to the unhewn forests, and brought forward, step by step, through the gradual processes of our ever-growing civilization, until we behold Toronto, the Queen City of a great Province, the centre of a thriving, populous agricultural district, a growing, stirring, unresting metropolis, the proud possessor of colleges of national repute, indomitable commercial pluck and enterprise, and vast material wealth."[55] It must have been a shock when the orator of the day, President Daniel Wilson of the University of Toronto, stated flatly, "that the history of the city was unwritten; in fact it had no history. It remained for the young men of to day to fill up the great white pages before them."[56] Instead of the usual comparisons with Chicago, Montreal, or Brooklyn, he spoke of Thebes, Jerusalem, and London. Wilson's views were not shared by most of Toronto. Books about past and present Toronto became popular, while artists depicted the juxtaposition of the old and new. In this drawing, history is represented by a dilapidated Fort York, progress by telegraph poles and the belching chimneys of factories. Toronto had begun as a military outpost; to its citizens it had become a commercial and industrial metropolis.

FAR AWAY FIELDS/1900-1929

CHAPTER THREE

"I admire Montreal, " wrote an English traveller in 1911, "but I simply fell head over heels in love with Toronto. It has a population of 350,000 progressive optimists. The whole city is full of bustle without hustle. It is a hive of healthy and vivacious industry.…Toronto, I say, breathes the spirit of progress and of the opening era – of the good new times."[57] Progressive optimists or not, the people of Toronto enjoyed good times in the early years of the century. The opening of the West was providing rich new markets, because the prairie farmer banked at branches of Toronto institutions, bought his goods from Eaton's catalogues, and harvested his grain with Massey-Harris equipment. Even more important was the discovery of the mineral resources of northern Ontario. "Cobalt built the St. Clair Avenue district, Noranda and Hollinger built Moore Park, and Nickel, Forest Hill."[58]

The Canadian Shield where the new riches were found was also of great importance in the development of art in Toronto. Before the first World War, several young Toronto artists became absorbed with the idea that Canadians should paint Canadian scenes in a distinctively Canadian way – "Canada painted in her own spirit."[59] They found their inspiration in the rocks and pines and muskegs of the Shield. The Studio Building, still standing in Rosedale Ravine, was built in 1914 for artists sharing this approach to their country and art. Dispersed during the first World War, the artists held their first joint exhibition in 1920, calling themselves the Group of Seven.

According to Lawren Harris, "The painters and their works were attacked from all sides.… The paintings were compared in the press to a 'Hungarian goulash,' 'a drunkard's stomach,' 'a head cheese' and so on."[60] Gradually, however, the Group won acceptance, and then great popularity. They painted from the Rocky Mountains to the Nova Scotian coast and north to the Arctic, but, except for Lawren Harris, they rarely painted Toronto. Many other artists followed their footsteps into the wilderness, and their influence on Canadian art was powerful. As one Toronto artist put it, "The Group of Seven was just coming into fashion. It made it difficult for some of us younger artists. I remember one conversation in particular where someone said that we would never be recognized as serious artists, because we couldn't paddle a canoe."[61]

The first World War disrupted the work of the Group of Seven, as it disrupted so many lives and hopes. In August 1914, while the Canadian National Exhibition prepared to open with its theme "Peace Year," the armouries were swamped with militia and volunteers. An estimated sixty thousand Toronto men – about one in nine of the population – served in the armed forces; about ten thousand died in the conflict. Artists recorded both the war itself and the home front, many of them as part of the Canadian War Records program.

Except for the war years, the tides of immigration continued to swell Toronto's population. In 1931 there were 631,207 people living in the city, among them many Jews, Italians, French, Germans, Poles, Dutch, Ukrainians and Finns. Both before and after the war many people came to Toronto from continental Europe because of economic conditions in their homeland or the dislocation of war. By 1931 almost one fifth of the population was of other than British origin. Toronto was still, nevertheless, fervently British – deliberately and self-consciously so, according to the English writer, Jan Morris. "It looked more or less like a bit of Birmingham, straightened out, and drained of bawdy and homogenized." Morris, however, thought that "by 1927 Toronto was willy-nilly diverging from its British patterns. For one thing it was far richer than any comparable British city of the homeland. It had far more cars, and many more telephones, and its commerce was run with more push and gusto."[62]

From the beginning, Toronto was a British city on North American soil, and was influenced by both ancestry and geography. In his history of Toronto, published in 1923, J. E. Middleton constantly commented on Toronto's Britishness, but he also wrote, "In outward semblance Toronto is an American city. Plate glass abounds. The shop windows are dressed in the alluring New York manner. The crowds are well-garbed and vivacious. The theatres and picture houses are served with plays and films from the United States....Poster advertising blossoms on every vacant lot or blank wall. The news-stands carry all the New York magazines. The multitudinous motor-cars are such as may be found on Woodward Avenue or State Street. At night the sky is aflame with advertising legends in electric lights. Even sky-scrapers have made their appearance. The downtown offices for the most part are luxurious palaces of marble and mahogany, with hardwood floors and beautiful lighting. Princesses innumerable inhabit them, clicking the keys of typewriters and adding machines with aristocratic fingers....The telephone is everywhere. The filing cabinet of American design is close at hand and the desk-top is likely to be covered with a sheet of plate glass – so that only the most surefooted flies dare light upon it."[63] In the 1920s and '30s, Toronto's basic dichotomy was very evident.

With its greatly increased population, Toronto needed more land. Between 1906 and 1912 it annexed a series of surrounding districts, in all about seventeen square miles, and built a number of bridges connecting the old and new parts of the city. "Within the present decade the city has crossed two rivers, marched up a hill, and clambered over two ravines, all of which give the residential region an aspect of romantic beauty."[64] Toronto now had an area of about thirty-five square miles and the approximate boundaries of the present city, except for Forest Hill and Swansea, added in 1967. The new land was not heavily populated, averaging about seven persons an acre; much of it was still farmers' fields, far from the centre of the city.

Farther away were the wheat fields of the West and the gold fields of the North, so important in Toronto's economic development. Farther away still, but close to the heart of Toronto, were the fields of Flanders, where thousands of Toronto's dead were buried beneath the poppies.

The *Globe* reviewer of the 1914 Royal Canadian Academy exhibition wrote that Gagen "strikes a new note in 'Temples of Commerce,' being an up-to-date study of part of Toronto's waterfront, with the skyscrapers piling up into a crescendo, the whole scene bathed in a beautiful, if somewhat exaggerated, rosy sunset glow."[65] The crescendo consisted of the Traders' Bank (1905) on the northeast corner of Yonge and Colborne Streets, and three new buildings at the Yonge and King Street intersection – the Dominion Bank (1914) on the southwest corner, the Canadian Pacific Building (1911-13) on the southeast corner, and the Royal Bank (1913-15) on the northeast corner. The Traders' Bank and later the Royal Bank were each in their day the tallest buildings in the British Empire. All four of Toronto's early skyscrapers are still standing, although they are dwarfed by much higher buildings to the west – the financial centre of the city has shifted towards Bay Street and beyond. The Board of Trade Building with its distinctive conical tower, on the northeast corner of Yonge and Front Streets, was torn down in the late 1950s. In the nineteenth century, pictures of Toronto showed the spires and towers of churches rising high above the city, but by 1914 temples of commerce rather than religion were beginning to dominate Toronto's skyline.

ROBERT F. GAGEN
Temples of Commerce, 1914
oil on canvas
68.3 x 101.4 cm.
MTL T30583

THOMAS G. GREENE *The Demolition of the "Ward"*, 1909   pen & ink over pencil   23.7 x 32.2 cm.   MTL T30343   Gift of L.R. MacTavish

THE DEMOLITION OF THE "WARD"

Eight acres of small houses and shops were cleared for the building of the Toronto General Hospital, opened in 1913 on College Street. They were in the northwest part of the "Ward," an unofficial area bounded by University Avenue, College, Yonge and Queen Streets, where many recent immigrants lived. It has been estimated that seventy per cent of the population of the "Ward" at this time was Jewish, fugitives from the pogroms of Eastern Europe. This sketch of the east side of Centre Street near Christopher Street was drawn to illustrate an article by Augustus Bridle, "The Drama of the 'Ward'," in the *Canadian Magazine*, Toronto, November, 1909, in which the demolition is described. "All the inhabitants, whether Jews or Gentiles, in that eight acres were given time to quit. They have quit. Their

walls are torn down. Even the little synagogue on one corner had to go. The houses were sold for a bagatelle each, to contractors to whom was given so much time to get them down and carted away. Gangs went in with crowbars and hammers. In a few days there was a large yawning desolation in that part of the ancient colony....Timbers hewn with the broadaxe seventy years ago were laid bare. Laths lay on the ground by carloads – firewood for the 'Ward'. Loads of lumber went rumbling out; loads of brick and of slate from the roofs on University Avenue, where some of the houses had brownstone fronts. The family cat sat blink-eyed among the ruins....Women and children came with toy waggons and baby carriages and aprons to take away the firewood."

ARTHUR H. HIDER *Joseph E. Seagram's Queen's and King's Plate Winners*, 1905 chromolithograph printed by Toronto Lithographing Co. 71 x 106.5 cm. MTL T13369

SEAGRAM'S PLATE WINNERS

Horse racing was popular in Toronto from the beginning of settlement, although there were occasional difficulties: for example, in 1837, "this day's sport was unfortunately interrupted in consequence of a decision of the Stewards being unpalatable to some interested persons who in revenge influenced the rabble to prevent further racing. The omission to provide a constabulary force was an unfortunate oversight."[66] In 1859 Queen Victoria presented the Queen's Plate of fifty guineas for Ontario-bred thoroughbreds that had never won a race, and the Queen's or King's Plate race has been run every year since 1860,

at first in Toronto and then elsewhere in Ontario. It returned permanently to Toronto in 1883, at Woodbine (now Greenwood) Race Track until 1955, and then at the new Woodbine Race Track in Etobicoke. Joseph E. Seagram, the Waterloo distiller, and the Seagram Stables that he founded, won the race twenty times, more than any other stable has ever done. This print, showing his eleven winners from 1891 to 1905 at Woodbine Race Track, was probably distributed to customers of Seagram's whiskey. It hung behind the bar in many Toronto taverns until they were closed by prohibition in 1916.

HENRY MARTIN *Ashbridge's Bay, Toronto*, ca 1900 watercolour 25.3 x 48.5 cm. Corporation of the City of Toronto

ASHBRIDGE'S BAY, TORONTO

The Don River originally entered Toronto Bay in a number of channels through an extensive marsh, with a narrow sand spit on the east connecting the Island with the mainland. Between the mainland and the Eastern Gap, permanently formed in 1858, lay a long marshy lagoon, called Ashbridge's Bay after a pioneer family who settled near it in the eighteenth century. In 1911 the City transferred Ashbridge's Bay and Marsh to the reorganized Toronto Harbour Commission, which created an industrial district with miles of railway tracks, paved streets, concrete piers and wharves. Ashbridge's Marsh had once been Toronto's most famous natural history landmark, particularly for migratory birds, but in the late 1950s the last sizable segment was filled in. The naturalist Fred Bodsworth commented, "The destruction of Ashbridge's Marsh is a sorry symbol of urban planners' blindness to natural features that give a region its distinctive quality. It is undisputed fact that Toronto needed Ashbridge's Marsh for harbour and industrial expansion – but did it need it *all*? Could not a few acres of the old cattail marsh have been preserved as a relic of the natural lakefront that is now gone, and as a haven for the birds and wildlife that were using it for thousands of years before man came?"[67]

J. McPHERSON ROSS *On the Beach, East Toronto*, n.d. oil on board 25.4 x 35.6 cm. Private Collection

"At that time there was no loose talk of the Beaches. There was Kew Beach, centred around Lee Avenue, and to the east was Balmy Beach – Bahmy to the purists, Bammy to the rest of us. And never the twain should meet, except at the annual regatta, as sworn enemies. An exaggeration, of course, but there was a certain feeling....In the summer of course there was bathing. Down the hill we went, my sister and I in scratchy lustre bathing suits, bloomers attached to a blouse with sailor collar (always the British Navy touch), skirt of decent length, stockings held up by round elastic garters, always too tight, one usually missing, and running shoes. My father and brother sported two-piece suits with blue and white horizontal stripes, elbow length sleeves and trunks to the knee. These immodest garments were well and truly concealed beneath heavy old raincoats, buttoned right up. Going down the hill was bad enough, but the climb up was Turkish bath torture. But it was worth it – clean water, cold indeed, but a good stretch of clean hot sand to warm us – which always involved still one more dip to rinse."[68] Mrs. Norman Keys thus described the Balmy Beach of her childhood. Her father, Senator John Lewis, moved with his family to the top of the hill on Spruce Hill Road in 1902, when Mrs. Keys was seven.

Steel was first used for construction in Chicago in the 1880s; combined with the electric elevator it made the building of skyscrapers possible. It was first used in Toronto in the Board of Trade Building (1888-91) and the Robert Simpson Company store (1892-94). By 1915 it was no longer a novelty, but people still watched as the steel girders – and the men working on them – climbed higher and higher. The Union Bank of Canada, founded in Quebec as the Union Bank of Lower Canada in 1865, had moved its head office to Winnipeg in 1912. It opened an office in Toronto in 1889, and in 1915 it erected a large building on the southeast corner of King and Bay Streets. At a time when so many Toronto firms were tapping the rich resources of the West, a Winnipeg bank was challenging Toronto at its financial heart. In 1925 the Union Bank merged with the Royal Bank of Canada. The artist is looking north from south of King Street, and shows the Mail Printing House on the northwest corner of King and Bay Streets.

ST. PATRICK'S MARKET

In 1836 D'Arcy Boulton Jr. of The Grange, who owned a hundred acres between Queen and Bloor Streets, gave the City a lot on Queen Street east of John Street to be used as a public market; eight years later he gave land for the Church of St. George the Martyr, seen here on the right. These gifts were made in the old tradition of the English landed gentry from which the Boulton family was descended, but there was probably also a more contemporary motive, since Boulton at the time was subdividing his property along Queen Street, and such amenities could increase the value of the lots offered for sale. The first market in what was then called West Toronto was a small frame building, named St. Patrick's because it was in St. Patrick's Ward. The building in the etching was designed by Thomas Young and replaced the first market in 1854. It was torn down in 1912.

OWEN STAPLES
Construction of the Union Bank, 1915
etching
20.3 x 16.5 cm.
AGO   Gift of the Artist, 1915

J. W. BEATTY
St. Patrick's Market, 1909
dry-point
14.9 x 21.9 cm.
MTL T11577

C. W. JEFFERYS *New Houses, Parkdale,* 1909 watercolour 25.5 x 28.7 cm.
AGO Gift of Mrs. K. W. Helm, daughter of C. W. Jefferys, Kneeland, California, 1980

NEW HOUSES, PARKDALE

In the 1870s Parkdale "sprang into existence" beyond Dufferin Street, the city's western boundary, and by 1878 "is rapidly growing and will soon become thickly inhabited and covered with charming villas."[69] Incorporated as a village in 1879 and as a town in 1886, Parkdale was annexed by Toronto in 1889. In 1893 Mazo de la Roche, aged fifteen, moved with her family to her grandfather's house on Dunn Avenue south of King Street. "The city seemed large to me, but compared with to-day how quiet, how peaceful, it must have been! My grandfather's house was in the west end, quite near the lake. Where there is now by the lake shore a railway line and apartment houses, there were fields of tall feathery grass and daisies which we children called marguerites. There were a few large houses with gardens by the lake. People of foreign birth were unknown there, with the exception of a Chinaman who kept a laundry and a long-bearded Jew with his cry of 'Rags – bones – bottles!' who drove a decrepit horse. My grandfather's house was one of five that stood on a tree-shaded street that ended in a kind of wooden terrace with seats, overlooking the lake. It had a deep stone porch where there were in this Maytime boxes filled with geraniums in bloom, lobelia and pansies. There were hanging baskets with already luxuriant growth."[70] By the first World War, Parkdale was almost completely built up, with many houses like the ones under construction here.

JOSEPH T. ROLPH *University Park near Technical School, Toronto,* June, 1911 watercolour 17.8 x 25.4 cm. Private Collection

UNIVERSITY PARK NEAR TECHNICAL SCHOOL

The Toronto Technical School was established by the City of Toronto in 1891 on the university campus. In 1900 it moved across College Street to the Stewart Building, originally the Toronto Athletic Club, and now occupied by the Ontario College of Art. Financed completely by the City, the Technical School provided free tuition in both day and night classes, and was operated by its own board, with representatives from the professional engineers' and architects' organizations, trade unions and manufacturers. This board amalgamated with the boards responsible for the public schools and for the collegiates to form the Toronto Board of Education in 1904; the Toronto Technical School was superceded by the Central Technical School opened by the new board in 1915. This view north of College Street across from the Technical School shows the group of private houses on the southeast corner of the university campus.

C. W. JEFFERYS
Morning Inspection, 1918
pencil
36.8 x 59.3 cm.
CWM/NMM/NMC 8245

MORNING INSPECTION

In July, 1917, No. 4 School of Military Aeronautics for members of the Royal Flying Corps Canada was established at the University of Toronto, where instruction was given on aircraft engines, rigging, wireless, artillery observation, machine guns, aircraft instruments and bombs. The cadets lived in Burwash Hall and the East Residence of Victoria College. They began their day with morning inspection on the back campus, with Wycliffe College Library on the left, the back of University College on the right, and a not completely finished Hart House behind the trees.

WOMEN OPERATORS

By 1916 the munitions factories were desperately short of labour, and in the autumn women were hired for the first time in this field. Hundreds of women waited outside the Toronto factories every morning, but this method of hiring was chaotic. In November, 1916, the Ontario Government opened the Women's Department of the Public Employment Bureau on Bay Street; in the beginning this system was also chaotic, because the Bureau was so swamped with applicants for work that its staff had no time to contact employers. Eventually, however, the Bureau sent thousands of Toronto women to the factories. In October, 1916, women began working night shifts in the munitions factories. Mark Irish of the Imperial Munitions Board wrote to the Chief Press Censor, "It is conceivable, but not probable, that some of these women or girls might be either actually, or in imagination, interfered with on the streets."[71] He requested that such incidents not be reported in the newspapers – the Censor agreed. The women in the painting are nose-boring and cutting off 9.2 inch shells in the Russell Motor Car works, on Weston Road in Toronto Junction. The Russell Motor Car Company was a subsidiary of the Canada Cycle & Motor Company (CCM) which had made the first Russell motor car in 1905. Toronto Junction developed around the intersection of the main lines of the Canadian National and Canadian Pacific Railways, and was heavily industrial because of the proximity of the tracks.

GEORGE A. REID
Women Operators, 1918
oil on canvas
121.9 x 168.3 cm.
CWM/NMM/NMC 8686

GEORGE A. REID "1917," 1917 pastel 47.3 x 63.5 cm. Central High School of Commerce TBE

"1917"

This sketch of Red Cross volunteers in the artist's studio was shown in the Ontario Society of Artists small pictures exhibition in 1917 and in the Royal Canadian Academy exhibition of 1918; a large oil painting based on it is in the Art Gallery of Ontario. In the first World War women followed their traditional roles of nursing, sewing, knitting, raising money and providing comforts for the men in the services and their families. J.E. Middleton commented, "Women who knit socks in public may have been a curiosity in 1915, but not in 1916."[72] For some women this was not enough. At least two women's rifle clubs were founded in Toronto by March, 1915, and in August, 1915, a

Women's Home Guard was unofficially organized in Toronto with four hundred recruits: "I got my rifle today and with it came one hundred rounds of ammunition. I'm loaded now."[73] The movement disintegrated less than six months later. Toronto newspapers considered the Guard as comic relief, possibly not in the best of taste. By 1916, however, an acute labour shortage necessitated a new role for women in offices, farms and factories. More than five hundred Toronto women were sent to camps at Clarkson, Oakville, Bronte and the Niagara Peninsula to pick fruit in the summer of 1917. Their greatest contribution to the labour force, however, was in the munitions factories.

J.E.H. MacDONALD *Tracks and Traffic*, 1912 oil on canvas 71.1 x 101.6 cm. AGO Gift of Walter C. Laidlaw, 1937

TRACKS AND TRAFFIC

"I first met MacDonald," Lawren Harris wrote, "at the old Arts and Letters Club in Toronto fifty years or more ago. There was an exhibition of his sketches on the walls of the club.... These sketches of MacDonald's affected me more than any painting I had ever seen in Europe. MacDonald and I became close friends. The two of us discussed the possibility of an art expression which should embody the moods and character and spirit of the country."[74] This meeting was of great importance in the development of the Group of Seven. MacDonald's exhibition was in November, 1911; that winter the two artists went sketching together. From their sketches on one such expedition to the foot of Bathurst Street, Harris painted *The Gas Works*, now in the Art Gallery of Ontario, and MacDonald his first important canvas, *Tracks and Traffic*, shown at the Ontario Society of Artists exhibition in 1912. Another version of this scene was painted by MacDonald on a bright sunny day.

SHIPBUILDING IN ASHBRIDGE'S BAY

The Polson Iron Works Company, founded in 1886, built a number of well known steamboats in Toronto, including *Knapp's Roller Boat* (1897) which was supposed to propel itself forward by constantly rolling over (it didn't), and the *Trillium* (1910) used for many years as a ferryboat to Toronto Island. Its shipyards at the foot of Sherbourne Street were very busy during the first World War, but were closed after the completion of wartime contracts in 1919. The ship on the stocks in the foreground of this picture is probably the *War Hydra*, a freighter commissioned by the Imperial Munitions Board on October 15, 1918 for wartime merchant service. Completed after the end of the war, she passed through a number of names and owners, until (as the Italian-owned *Nina Bianchi*) she was finally sunk in a collision in the Mediterranean in 1940. Polson's built eight of these freighters for Great Britain; a total of twenty-four were built on the Great Lakes, including the *War Ontario* and the *War Toronto* built by the Toronto Shipbuilding Company at its shipyards on Keating Channel.

AEROPLANE FACTORY, READY FOR SHIPMENT

In 1915 the American firm, Curtiss Company, established an aeroplane factory on Strachan Avenue. Taken over by the Imperial Munitions Board in 1917 and renamed Canadian Aeroplanes Ltd., it was the only such factory in Canada during the first World War. A huge new plant covering six acres was built very quickly on the west side of Dufferin Street south of Dupont Street. Working twenty-four hours a day in two shifts (twelve hours each, with half an hour for lunch), the plant turned out more than 2900 Curtiss JN4 training planes in two years. In April, 1918, it received a contract from the United States Navy for thirty twin-engined F5 flying boats; with a wingspan of 102 feet, these were the largest aeroplanes yet built in North America. The first F5 was completed three months later, and all thirty were delivered within seven months. This view, in Factory No. 2, shows one of the flying-boats ready for shipment.

ROBERT F. GAGEN
Shipbuilding in Ashbridge's Bay, Toronto, 1918
oil on canvas
144.8 x 205.7 cm.
CWM/NMM/NMC 8167

DOROTHY STEVENS
Aeroplane Factory, Ready for Shipment, 1918
etching
30.2 x 37.9 cm.
CWM/NMM/NMC 8826

At the outbreak of war, there was an immediate need for military hospitals, which became urgent as the wounded were sent home from overseas. The first military hospital in Toronto was opened at Exhibition Camp in the CNE grounds in 1914, and in 1916 the old Toronto General Hospital on Gerrard Street, previously used as a barracks, became the Base Hospital. Still more beds were needed; in May, 1917, the Orthopaedic Military Hospital opened in the Salvation Army's new Booth Memorial building on Davisville Avenue just west of Mount Pleasant Road, with 180 beds and an artificial limb factory. This painting shows some of its patients at the corner of Yonge Street and Davisville Avenue – "wizz bang corner" according to the graffiti on the wall. In the foreground is the verandah of an hotel built by the Davis family in the first half of the nineteenth century and burned down in the 1920s; across Davisville Avenue is a grocery store from the same period, still operated by Davises in 1918, and still standing in 1983. John Davis came to Canada in 1840, and established a pottery on the east side of Yonge Street north of Davisville Avenue. He and his family owned most of the land around the intersection, which became known as Davisville. In 1889 the unincorporated villages of Davisville and Eglinton with their immediate neighbourhoods were incorporated as the Village of North Toronto. Its boundaries were extended when it became the Town of North Toronto in 1890, with a population of about a thousand. In 1912 North Toronto, with more than six thousand people, was annexed by the City of Toronto.

STANLEY F. TURNER
A War Record, ca 1918
tempera on board
66.2 x 96.6 cm.
CWM/NMM/NMC 8907

"Toronto was awakened from its slumbers at 2:55 o'clock this morning," reported the *Globe* on November 11, 1918. "The first flash bulletin that armistice had been signed came through over the Associated Press wires to the newspapers at that hour. Within a few minutes many whistles in all parts of the city were blowing full blast. Eaton's big 'wildcat' siren awakened the whole city. Toronto citizens rubbed their eyes and could not believe their senses. The newspaper offices were swamped with telephone calls. At a little after 3 o'clock a procession, mostly of women munition workers, paraded Yonge Street, cheering, wildly beating tin pans and blowing whistles. By this time a crowd began to gather all along Yonge Street, motor cars came tearing down street, reckless of all speed laws, tooting their horns and awakening the entire city." This painting shows the crowds on Yonge Street north of King Street. On the right is the Royal Bank building, standing on the northeast corner of Yonge and King Streets.

J. ERNEST SAMPSON
Armistice Day, Toronto, ca 1918
oil on linen
152.8 x 91.7 cm.
CWM/NMM/NMC 8795

STANLEY F. TURNER
Construction of the Bloor Street Viaduct, ca 1918
etching
26.2 x 14.6 cm.
AGO Gift of Sir Edmund Walker Estate, 1928

CONSTRUCTION OF BLOOR STREET VIADUCT

For most of the nineteenth century Danforth Road was a dusty country lane through open fields and market gardens, with an occasional hotel or small factory. The only adequate bridge across the Don River was at Queen Street, so that the Danforth district was effectively cut off from the city. In 1913, after two previous rejections, a plebiscite approved spending two and a half million dollars to bridge the broad river valley at Bloor Street, and construction began in January, 1915. The Bloor Street Viaduct (renamed the Prince Edward Viaduct in 1919 in honour of the Prince of Wales, later King Edward VIII), is almost a third of a mile long. It was designed to carry pedestrians, vehicular traffic, a streetcar line, a water main (which was never built), and a subway line (which opened in 1966). Work on the viaduct continued throughout the war, and was watched with interest by a young Gordon Sinclair and his friends, who lived near Riverdale Zoo. When they saw that the spans on either side were joined by two planks, five of them decided that they would be the first to walk across; all went well until the fifth boy froze in terror, lying on the planks and refusing to move, but eventually he too crawled to safety. Thus the bridge across the Don was opened. Finally completed in 1918, the viaduct stimulated a period of spectacular growth "out the Danforth."

GERMAN SUBMARINE COMING THRO' CUT

The German submarine UC-97 was one of five surrendered U-boats handed over by the British Admiralty to the United States after the first World War. Manned by the United States Navy and accompanied by the U.S. tug *Iroquois,* it steamed through the Eastern Gap into Toronto Harbour on June 11, 1919, on its way to Chicago. It "was greeted on all sides with the acclamation of diving aeroplanes, city factory whistles, whistles from all water craft, motorboats, small craft, and a thousand or so citizens who lined the Harbor Commission dock to welcome the vessel at her berth."[75] Another copy of this etching in the Canadian War Museum (8332) is called "Toronto city officials escorting the first German submarine in Canadian waters."

F. W. JOPLING
German submarine coming thro' cut for first in Toronto,
June 11, 1919
etching
29 x 52.2 cm.
MTL T13217

LAWREN HARRIS *The Eaton Manufacturing Building*, 1911 oil on canvas 76.2 x 75 cm.
Archives, Eaton's of Canada

EATON MANUFACTURING BUILDING

Timothy Eaton immigrated to Canada from Ireland in 1854; after shopkeeping in several small Ontario towns, he came to Toronto in 1869, and opened a store on Yonge Street. This store was extremely successful, as was the mail-order business he began with his first catalogue in 1884. The T. Eaton Company started to manufacture its own goods in 1890, building over the years a number of factories behind the store north of the old City Hall. This view looks east towards Factory No. 4, built in 1909-10 on the west side of Downey's Lane north of Louisa Street. Except for two floors, this building was devoted to the production of ready-made clothing. Although working conditions in the garment industry were generally very poor, those at Eaton's were better than average. The majority of workers were recently arrived Eastern European Jews living in the "Ward." In the decade before the first World War, Eaton's was the largest single employer of Jewish labour in Toronto; it was one of the few factories that did not insist on Saturday work. In 1912, however, there was an unsuccessful strike at Eaton's clothing factory over a number of grievances, but the basic issue was unionization. One of Harris' few pictures of industrial buildings, this painting was shown at the Ontario Society of Artists exhibition in 1912.

LAWREN HARRIS *Houses, Richmond Street,* 1911 oil on canvas 76.2 x 81.2 cm. The Arts and Letters Club, Toronto

"Surely there is scarcely a spot in Toronto's streets where trees in abundance do not meet the eye. The chestnut is by long odds the favourite, though the elm, the poplar, the oak and Canada's own maple are by no means wanting. The more fashionable thoroughfares are lined with them, while the less pretentious by-ways, the home of the artisan and the mechanic, give goodly promise of refreshing greenery in the near future, even every bandbox of a cottage having before it its sapling or two and its bits of boulevard."[76] Written in 1885, this has always been true of Toronto's residential streets, although the horse chestnut has become much less common, and street widening, pollution, and the Dutch elm disease have all taken their toll.

This painting was first shown at the Ontario Society of Artists exhibition in 1922. The *Globe* review commented on the "subtle sentiment" that conveyed "with much feeling the squalid surroundings of an old house in the slum district,"[77] but the *Telegram* reviewer was more critical. "Canadian art is indeed indebted to the artist for this record of what happened to the fence in the rear of the home of Mr. Two Dimensions during the coal strike, also for the domestic hint that if washing is suspended from the second storey it is less liable to the depredations of line robbers. This painting is much admired – by some people, which suggests that the less one knows of artists, the better you can arrive at an unprejudiced opinion about art."[78] Even in this somewhat sombre painting, Harris presents an antiseptic and stylized view of slums; he does not include most of the details he describes in his poem, "A Question" published in 1922:

> Lanes littered with ashes, boxes, cans, old rags;
> Dirty, musty, garbage-reeking lanes
> Behind the soot-dripped backs of blunt houses,
> Sour yards and slack-sagging fences...[79]

Church Street Public School was opened in 1872 in a four-room building in the middle of the fields near the present corner of Church and Alexander Streets. This building burned down in the 1880s, and was replaced in 1891. The second school, with an addition in 1920, lasted until 1957, when both it and the Wellesley Public School were replaced by the present building. This view of the boys' playground shows typical boys' clothing in the late 1920s. Of the three in the foreground, the boy on the left wears the outsize cap and breeches popular in North America, while the little one in the middle looks like an English schoolboy, and the boy on the right is more casually dressed. Like several of the other boys, he wears a leather aviator's helmet, which became a craze after Charles Lindbergh's solo flight across the Atlantic in 1927.

LAWREN HARRIS
Morning, ca 1921
oil on canvas
97.1 x 112.4 cm.
Beaverbrook Art Gallery, Fredericton, N.B.
Gift of the W. Garfield Weston Foundation

D. McINTOSH PATERSON
Schoolyard at Recess, ca 1929
watercolour over pencil
43.2 x 55.8 cm.
ROM CC   Gift of D.A. Paterson

LAWREN HARRIS *Old Houses, Toronto, Winter,* 1919 oil on canvas 82.6 x 98.1 cm.
AGO Gift of the Canadian National Exhibition Association, 1965

OLD HOUSES, TORONTO, WINTER

This picture, shown at the Ontario Society of Artists exhibition in 1919 as "In the Ward III," is typical of Harris' paintings of houses at the end of the first World War. It lacks the idyllic charm of earlier paintings, like his *Houses, Richmond Street,* but at the same time does not have "the alienated impersonality"[80] of his later *Morning.* Although the houses are obviously slums, there is almost a gaiety about the picture. As the Jews moved westward out of the "Ward," other recent immigrants took their places. In the 1911 census there were 472 Blacks in Toronto, most of them born in Canada, many tracing their ancestry back to the Underground Railway days before the American Civil War. During the first World War and immediately afterwards, a number of British West Indians settled in Toronto, many of them working on the railways and in the service trades. By the 1921 census there were 1236 Blacks in the city. They were scattered in the central downtown areas; according to Harry Gairey, who came to Toronto from Jamaica via Cuba in 1914, "A few coloured people lived on Adelaide Street, a few on Queen Street, some in Cabbagetown and on University Avenue."[81] All three Black churches, however, were in the "Ward" at this time.

LAWREN HARRIS *Winter Afternoon*, 1918 oil on canvas 102.9 x 114.3 cm. Private Collection

WINTER AFTERNOON

Lawren Harris painted many pictures of Toronto houses, between 1909 and 1926. Most of them were of houses in the "Ward," or in the Earlscourt area (now in the city of York) described by Harris as "a picturesque semi-slum district west of Bathurst and south of Eglington."[82] This painting, one of the few painted in the more prosperous parts of the city, depicts a house on Avenue Road, a block or two north of Bloor Street. Some of the largest houses in the Annex and Yorkville were in this neighbourhood: for example, Sir William Mortimer Clark's big stone house was on the corner of Avenue Road and Prince Arthur Avenue. There were also a number of houses in the style of the one in the painting; in 1983 only one remains.

MIDWINTER

This view shows typical Toronto middle-class houses, probably in the west end of the city, since the artist was living on Indian Road and teaching at Western Technical School when the picture was painted. Many areas of Toronto still look like this: although there have been radical changes in the last sixty years, there have also been continuity and stability, as small parts of Toronto remain untouched by the passage of time, except for the ubiquitous automobile and television aerial. In 1923 J.E. Middleton wrote, "The pride of Toronto is in the infinity of moderate-sized houses, nearly all of brick, and for the most part faced by well-kept lawns and flower gardens."[83] This painting was shown at the Ontario Society of Artists exhibition in 1926.

SUNNYSIDE, TORONTO

Sunnyside Amusement Park, opened in June, 1922, was constructed by the Toronto Harbour Commission on land filled in as a major work project a few years earlier. Operated by the Sunnyside Amusement Company, it had two merry-go-rounds, a ferris wheel, a roller-coaster called the Sunnyside Flyer, a bandshell called the Orthophonic, swimming and dance pavilions, games of chance and other midway attractions. The two-mile-long boardwalk had been built long before the amusement park, and was a popular promenade; for years Toronto's Easter Parade was held at Sunnyside. As part of its relief program during the depression, the City built a new boardwalk in 1934; this was the period when Sunnyside was called "the unemployed man's Riviera." The sandy beach shown here, lay between the boardwalk and the lake. Lakeshore Boulevard, then Toronto's main route westward, ran through the amusement park, which created a bottleneck for the increasingly heavy traffic; Sunnyside was torn down in 1956. All that remains are the Palais Royale Ballroom, a refreshment booth, and the Sunnyside Bathing Pavilion, with its sgraffito gold and blue porpoises and sea-monsters above the entrance, designed by the artist James Blomfield.

L.A.C. PANTON
Midwinter, ca 1926
oil on canvas
87.6 x 101.6 cm.
National Gallery of Canada, Ottawa

MARY E. WRINCH
Sunnyside, Toronto, 1923
oil on canvas
91.4 x 100.3 cm.
National Gallery of Canada, Ottawa

St. Olave's Anglican Church was built in 1887 on Windermere Avenue north of the present Queensway. It was a simple roughcast building which could accommodate 115 people; the congregation moved to its present location just south of Bloor Street in 1926. The land for the original church was given by the proprietor of the Swansea Bolt Works and Rolling Mills, founded at the foot of Windermere Avenue in 1882. The first Anglican services in Swansea were held in the Bolt Works, which played an important role in the development of the area. Further north, houses were built in the late 1880s around the experimental gardens of the seedsman William Rennie, while Home Smith and Company bought land along the Humber River in 1911, and opened its first subdivision there, Riverside, in 1913. The Village of Swansea, bounded by Bloor Street, Grenadier Pond, the Canadian National Railways tracks, and the Humber River, was incorporated in 1926. In 1953 it was the smallest partner in the new Municipality of Metropolitan Toronto, with a population of about eight thousand. Swansea became part of the City of Toronto on January 1, 1967. It has given the city two mayors – David Crombie (1972-78), and the present incumbent, Arthur Eggleton.

HOUSETOPS IN THE WARD

The ideal home of the average middle-class Torontonian of the 1920s was red brick, foursquare, solid, and uncompromising. Every third year or so the verandah and trim were painted dark green sometimes with white, or dark brown sometimes with cream. Even the very popular Tudor style houses that several developers were building, among them Home Smith in Swansea and across the Humber River, were black and white, or dark brown and cream. It was only in the areas where recent immigrants lived, such as the slums of the "Ward," that houses were brightly painted. In this view from above their snow-covered roofs, the charm and gaiety of their vivid colours mask their poverty.

A. J. CASSON
Old Church, Swansea, 1920
oil on board
24 x 29.9 cm.
Mr. and Mrs. David Sharpe

A. J. CASSON
Housetops in the Ward, 1924
oil on canvas
114.3 x 94 cm.
Private Collection

OPENING OF THE WALKER COURT

In 1900 the Art Museum of Toronto was incorporated; its name was changed to the Art Gallery of Toronto in 1919, and to the Art Gallery of Ontario in 1966. Its first permanent exhibition rooms were opened in 1913 in the Boulton family's old house, The Grange, bequeathed for that purpose by Mrs. Goldwin Smith. In 1918 three new galleries were opened north of The Grange, and in 1926 the Walker Court with the Fudger and Leonard Galleries on each side. The Walker Court, named after the Gallery's first president, Sir Edmund Walker, has been used ever since for the display of sculpture, and for receptions and concerts. Many new galleries and facilities were opened at the Art Gallery in 1977, but the Walker Court is still at the heart of the building. Owen Staples was for many years a staff artist for the *Evening Telegram*. This sketch illustrated R. McEvoy's story, "Gala Opening of Toronto's New Palace of Art," in the *Telegram* of January 30, 1926, which described "a scene of light, music, and animation such as even the Boulton days never knew."

WATERFRONT, EAST TORONTO

In the nineteenth century the port of Toronto had been very busy, but by 1900 its harbour facilities had become inadequate. Vessels had difficulty finding a suitable wharf, despite the multiplicity of private wharves along the waterfront – there were forty between Bathurst and Parliament Streets in 1908. Ships became grounded in the mud of the undredged harbour. The grain elevators of both the Grand Trunk and the Northern Railways had been destroyed by fire. In 1911 a new Toronto Harbour Commission was established to have jurisdiction over the whole harbour area, planning and controlling its develop-ment both for industrial and recreational purposes. A vast scheme of dredging, land reclamation and building was begun. By 1930 the harbour was rapidly being transformed into a modern port. All the waterfront buildings in this painting of the eastern end of the harbour were demolished in the late 1920s. The old Gooderham and Worts grain elevator in the foreground had not been used for many years.

OWEN STAPLES
Formal Opening of the New Sir Edmund Walker Court, 1926
pen & ink on card with touches of gouache
35.6 x 70.5 cm.
AGO Gift of a member of the Women's Committee, 1970

RICHARD MAJOR
Waterfront, East Toronto, 1924
gouache on board
26.5 x 21.5 cm.
Corporation of the City of Toronto

DEPRESSION, WAR, RECOVERY/1930-1953

CHAPTER FOUR

"I was able to get a job where some of them weren't. But I tramped the whole city of Toronto on foot – I couldn't afford a car-fare – before I did get a job. I shovelled ditches on Cherry Street down there when they were startin' to build that and pave it."[84] Although individuals and families had experienced bleak poverty throughout the city's history, there had been nothing like the massive depression that followed the stock market crash of 1929. At one point in 1934 there were almost a hundred and twenty thousand people on relief in Toronto. Many were ashamed of being on welfare: for example, women receiving food at the House of Industry "would come with baby carriages and cover up the groceries they got with a shawl so that no one would know, so that no one could see the brown paper bags."[85] After 1933 weekly vouchers were issued, but "the meat voucher serves for only one or two meals; hence the relief recipients are practising vegetarians most of the week."[86] Toronto with its diversified economy did not suffer as much as some of the less fortunate areas, but on the other hand, it attracted many transients from across the country, who hoped that somewhere in the big city there would be work.

Like everyone else, artists in Toronto were affected by the depression. Carl Schaefer, for example, supported his family by part-time teaching in the winters, spending the summers on his grandfather's farm. Despite Paraskeva Clark's rousing call to "come out from behind the Pre-Cambrian Shield,"[87] Toronto artists rarely expressed social or political opinion in their paintings. When Clark arrived in the city in 1931 she said "it was a dead place. Nothing but Group of Seven...the bloody Group of Seven. Nothing but landscape, landscape, landscape."[88] Although the Group of Seven disbanded in 1933 when the larger Canadian Group of Painters was formed, the emphasis on landscape painting remained. Toronto artists ranged throughout Canada looking for suitable subjects; not many painted Toronto itself. The most complete record of the city in this period comes from the print-makers, whose etchings, woodcuts and aquatints depicted Toronto streets and buildings.

The outbreak of war in 1939 ended the depression, as industries swung into war production and men and women enlisted in the armed forces. As in the first World War, a number of Toronto artists, including Aba Bayefsky, Rowley Murphy and Carl Schaefer, served in the forces as official war artists. Others continued to paint in the city, among them David Milne, who spent a year in Toronto in 1939-40. "Most of this time I have been in Toronto and painting just about as usual. Only instead of rocks and bays and bush the subjects have been living rooms and dining rooms and kitchens, streets and docks and churches. I am expecting arrest almost any time for drawing down along the waterfront and industrial area, but so far nothing has happened."[89] His son commented, "He got the same interest and kick viewing piles of coal and oil tanks on the Toronto waterfront as he had from sunsets or the turning leaves."[90]

After the end of the war there was a period of economic dislocation while business and industry returned to peacetime conditions. There was also an acute housing shortage, worse than after the first World War because there had been little construction during the depression. Accommodation was still scarce when the first waves of post-war immigration reached Toronto. Immigration had been restricted during the depression and virtually impossible during the war; after 1945 thousands of immigrants came to Toronto, many of them from the refugee camps of Europe. In 1951 the population of Toronto was 675,754, with less than seventy per cent of British origin. The newcomers brought with them different traditions and experiences, greatly enriching the city.

Despite this immigration, between 1945 and 1950 the population of Toronto declined for the first time. The number of people in the city dropped by more than two per cent, while the population of the neighbouring municipalities increased tremendously: for example, North York grew by 137 per cent, and Etobicoke by 106 per cent. "Over to the East lay the Golden Mileage of Scarboro and the new suburbia: the meadows of apartment houses, the forests of aluminum lamp standards and a desert of asphalt with the oasis of a shopping centre at its heart."[91] The great move to the suburbs had begun.

For many years there had been people working in the city but living beyond its limits, usually because of cheaper land and lower taxes. Some lived outside the city because less stringent building codes made it possible to build their own houses by stages as finances permitted, others because they were attracted by the combination of semi-rural and semi-urban conditions. The post-war move to the suburbs was different. Instead of a few hundreds, there were now thousands of people anxious to find homes. Acres of land were subdivided by developers who built houses and apartments, row on row, block on block. Most of the people who moved into these subdivisions could not find accommodation within the city itself.

By 1950 the city of Toronto was more or less saturated as a residential area, even with its new high-rise apartments. It was surrounded by twelve municipalities with widely varying populations, assessments and services. In 1953 the Province of Ontario established a new system of government for the two hundred and forty square miles of metropolitan area. The new Municipality of Metropolitan Toronto was to be governed by representatives of the city and suburbs, and to be responsible for such matters as public transportation where co-ordination was essential. The thirteen municipalities would retain jurisdiction over more local concerns. In 1953 the City of Toronto and its suburban partners thus entered a new era.

Because of the city's terrain, it has always been difficult to get an overall view of Toronto. In the late nineteenth century when bird's-eye views were popular, big chromolithographs were published of the entire city, usually from an imaginary vantage-point high above the lake. The draftsman's aim was to produce an exact topographical picture, including recognizable portraits of all the larger buildings and even some of the houses. In this century few artists have attempted general views of Toronto, although photographers have assiduously climbed tall buildings and peered out of aeroplanes to record city-wide vistas. "The site of Toronto is such that you can't see it," wrote Stephen Leacock. "When you are downtown you can't see uptown and when you are uptown you can't see downtown and both uptown and downtown you can't see sideways. The reason is that the main part of the city occupies a very mean elevation, rising a few feet from the level of the Bay…and not rising any more for two miles, then meeting a hill a hundred feet high, lifting itself to the top of that, and then falling flat again. A noble view is obtained from the Oak Ridges twenty miles north extending in very clear weather right across Lake Ontario; but this view doesn't include Toronto and Toronto doesn't get this view."[92] In this print the artist has depicted the downtown area from above Church Street north of Shuter Street. St. Michael's Cathedral and Metropolitan United Church are in the foreground; further south are the King Edward Hotel, the Royal Bank, the Dominion Bank, the Canadian Bank of Commerce and the Royal York Hotel.

NICHOLAS HORNYANSKY
Snowbound Downtown, 1938
colour aquatint
11.4 x 13.1 cm.
MTL T10321

ROWLEY MURPHY
East Side, Old York Street, 1930-36
watercolour
54 X 73.7 cm.
AGO

EAST SIDE, OLD YORK STREET

By the 1880s, the east side of York Street between King and Queen Streets had become a slum. Mulvany in 1884 wrote that "the eastern side is occupied by dingy and rotten shanties."[93] By the 1930s, all the old buildings between Queen and Richmond Streets were occupied by second-hand stores, except for one lunch counter. This painting is of the block below Richmond Street, and shows what was then called a "parking yard," Adolph Rosenthal's second-hand book shop, Jean Osler's second-hand store, John H. Clarke's cigar store, and William P. Moore's barber shop. This section of York Street was a popular subject with artists because of the contrast between its poverty and the new high buildings behind it on Bay Street.

STREET EXTENSION

By the end of the 1920s, traffic congestion began to be a serious problem, with more than 93,000 cars crowding streets designed before the age of the automobile. University Avenue originally ended at Queen Street; its extension southward had been suggested in 1918 as a war memorial. In 1929 the Advisory City Planning Commission produced its proposal. The extension was to connect a large circular plaza at Richmond Street, to be called Vimy Circle, with an open space at Front and York Streets, to be called Britannia Square. The provincial war memorial was to be erected in the centre of Vimy Circle, while the design of all the new buildings was to be strictly controlled, and overhead wires, billboards, and illuminated signs forbidden. Unfortunately, the depression made this grand Beaux Arts plan impracticable. After the demolition of many buildings, the University Avenue extension was built without any of the proposed embellishments, and was completed in 1931. The Canadian Pacific Railway's Royal York Hotel, opened in 1929, was the biggest hotel in the British Empire. For a time it was surpassed by the Canadian National Railways' Queen Elizabeth Hotel (Le Reine Élizabeth) in Montreal, but it regained its title by adding a new wing in 1959. With sixteen hundred rooms, the Royal York is still one of the world's largest hotels.

ANDRÉ LAPINE
Street Extension, ca 1931
watercolour
48.9 x 35.1 cm.
AGO

GORDON WEBBER *Skating in the Park*, 1933-34 oil on cardboard 45.7 x 55.9 cm. AGO

SKATING IN THE PARK

This rink in Grange Park south of the Art Gallery of Ontario was typical of many scattered throughout the city in parks, backyards and vacant lots. Small boys skating here in the 1930s dreamed of their heroes – Charlie Conacher, Busher Jackson, King Clancy and the other Maple Leafs – who won their first Stanley Cup in 1932, the season in which Maple Leaf Gardens was opened. In the depths of the depression most boys had little hope of seeing the games at the Gardens, but all Toronto listened to Foster Hewitt's radio broadcasts, and Saturday night was hockey night in Canada to a whole generation.

ISABEL McLAUGHLIN *Backyards*, 1933   oil on canvas   66 x 66 cm.   Collection of the Artist

BACKYARDS

This view of the backyards of houses on Asquith Avenue is from the artist's studio above the former Royal Bank branch on the northeast corner of Bloor and Yonge Streets. When Yorkville was subdivided, the present Asquith Avenue was called Jarvis Street, but when the village became part of Toronto the name was changed to Bismarck Avenue after Germany's Iron Chancellor, to avoid confusion with the city's Jarvis Street. In 1915 the sinking of the *Lusitania* inflamed anti-German feeling: for example, Mayor T. L. Church ordered the removal of an electric sign advertising German beer made in Berlin, Ontario. A month later this order was rescinded on the advice of the City Solicitor, and a year later Berlin was renamed Kitchener in honour of the British military leader. Street names with German associations were changed, among them Bismarck Avenue, which became Asquith Avenue after the then British Prime Minister.

CORRY W. BRIGDEN
Lower Bay Street, 1934
woodblock
11.3 x 16 cm.
(from the portfolio *Toronto, Old and New*) AGO

"Bay St. *is* Toronto," wrote Ron Haggart in 1965. "It is a crowded, hectic, uncomfortable street. You cannot stroll on its sidewalks. You will be trampled underfoot. It is the street of green-carpeted loan companies; of lawyers in one tower making excuses for mining promoters in another; the street where the stock exchange traders with their red-and-white lapel buttons bark huskily for a drug store coffee before going back to shout up the value of whatever northern muskeg was promoted in this week's tip sheet. And it is one of the few streets in Toronto…where you can actually see what a building looks like."[94] The building you can see is the old City Hall, designed by E.J. Lennox and still standing proudly at the head of lower Bay Street. A proposal that it be torn down when the present City Hall was built aroused a public outcry; the old building was not only preserved but restored to some of its earlier grandeur. There were three public ceremonies connected with its building; the first was the laying of a six-ton cornerstone in 1891, and the second the laying of the last stone on top of the tower in 1898, with the official party hoisted aloft in a flag-draped bucket. Finally on September 18, 1899, the City Hall was officially opened.

OLD CITY HALL MEWS

Before the 1960s, the site of the present City Hall and Nathan Phillips Square was a tangle of old decrepit buildings. Several small streets ran through the area, where the only large buildings were Shea's Hippodrome on Bay Street, which had been one of Toronto's most famous vaudeville houses before becoming a movie theatre, and the Registry Office further west. Along Queen Street was a row of low ramshackle shops, most of them occupied by pawnbrokers or second-hand dealers. On Albert Street there was a plumbing and heating business beside a lumberyard, while Elizabeth and Chestnut Streets were part of Chinatown. Scattered through the area were a number of shabby cottages. The artist shows the tower of the old City Hall rising above this labyrinth of old buildings.

NICHOLAS HORNYANSKY
Old City Hall Mews, 193–?
colour aquatint
16 x 10.5 cm.
Mr. and Mrs. W. Tennison
and Family,
Maydwell Manufacturing Co. Ltd.

THE CANADIAN BANK OF COMMERCE BUILDING

"That white palace soaring aloft five hundred feet is not a Bank," wrote J.E. Middleton, "it is a Bank Building....The building is an expression of the Bank and its policy."[95] Every generation in Toronto seems to put up at least one new building on a much larger scale than any previous building in the city. Sometimes its predominance is short-lived, like that of the Toronto-Dominion Centre's Bank Tower; others dominate the skyline for years, like the Canadian Bank of Commerce Head Office on King Street west of Bay Street. Designed by the New York firm of York and Sawyer, its erection in 1929-31 was supervised by Toronto's Darling and Pearson. Toronto's first real skyscraper with thirty-four storeys, it was the tallest building in the British Empire for many years. Now part of the Commerce Court complex, it is dwarfed by many of its neighbours.

ALONG THE WATERFRONT, TORONTO HARBOUR

After the first World War, Toronto's harbour was greatly improved and its use increased sharply. In 1933 more than two and a half million tons of cargo passed through the harbour, with incoming cargoes, as usual, far greater than outgoing ones. The largest vessels on the Great Lakes could be accommodated, but until the opening of the St. Lawrence Seaway in 1959 there was little ocean shipping. In 1933, however, thirty-one small ocean freighters did come directly to Toronto from eleven different European and Pacific ports. On one red-letter day, "five ocean freighters of different nationalities were docked in Toronto Harbour, and small though they were, their flags gave Toronto the air of an Ocean port."[96]

WOODRUFF KERR AYKROYD
The Canadian Bank of Commerce Building, 1933
etching
24.8 x 18.6 cm.
Corporation of the City of Toronto

HARRY DRAPER WALLACE
Along the Waterfront, Toronto Harbour, 1932
etching
21.3 x 26.7 cm.
Corporation of the City of Toronto
Gift of Mrs. Claire Brooks

CARL SCHAEFER *Moon over the Don Jail*, 1938   watercolour   50.2 x 57.2 cm.   Private Collection

The artist, who was living on Bain Avenue near the Don Jail, wrote of this painting, "One evening walking home from Central Technical School where I had a class, along Gerrard Street East, turning north up Broadview, there it was! I'd really seen it for the first time. Under a romantic night sky with slow moving clouds and a pale moon, that great gray fortress, ominous and grim. I made a pencil scribble on the back of a cigarette box and painted it out of my head the next day."[97] He later discovered that Morley Callaghan had described the same view in the opening chapter of his novel, *It's Never Over* (1930). Callaghan wrote of the crowd gathered outside the jail on the night before a hanging. "The people standing under the trees were staring at the cell window, pointing, talking rapidly without looking at each other....A broad-shouldered man, his arms linked behind him, standing on tiptoes, suddenly shouted: 'There he is!'....All the faces were lifted to him, and now he was pressing his own face against the bars as if it had become very important that he should not miss a single movement or fail to see a single upturned face. The eager movements, the faces lifted up to him and the small cheer were the movements and rhythm in a brief new world, important in every detail because he had an immediate relation with everything in it. Everything for the moment belonged to him. The face never moved behind the bars, and was always turned at the same angle, the neck craning toward the crowd."[98] The last executions in Canada were the hanging of two men at the Don Jail in 1962.

JACK BUSH *The Armories, Toronto*, 1939 oil on board 21.6 x 27.3 cm. Mr. Mendy Sharf

THE ARMORIES, TORONTO

At the outbreak of war in September, 1939, there was immediate mobilization, and Toronto's old armouries on University Avenue became intensely busy. Designed by Thomas Fuller, they were built by the Department of Public Works in 1891-93 to house the Toronto militia regiments. A number of these distinctive castle-like buildings were erected in cities and towns across Canada at this period; the Toronto armouries were the largest in Canada, with an immense drill hall spanned by steel vaulting supported only by the outside walls. They were used during the Boer War and the two World Wars, as well as for the training of the peacetime militia. In 1963 they were torn down to make room for the new provincial Court House. In the second World War, thousands of Toronto citizens joined the Royal Canadian Navy, the Canadian Army, and the Royal Canadian Air Force; they saw action in theatres of combat around the world. The City of Toronto's Book of Remembrance in the rotunda of City Hall preserves the names of 3264 men and women who died in the conflict.

AT DRY DOCK

The little wooden tug, *Elsie Doris*, was built at Midland in 1921 for the Ontario Department of Mines. Bought by the Toronto Dry Dock Company in the 1930s, she became a familiar sight in the harbour. When work on the Island Airport began in 1937, trucks and heavy equipment had to be transported to the site from the mainland. For many months the *Elsie Doris* pushed scows back and forth, back and forth, from the foot of Spadina Avenue. She was broken up in 1945, but her melodious three-part chime whistle is still preserved in the Marine Museum. She is shown at the Toronto Dry Dock Company's wharf on Keating Channel.

FORGE SHOP

This forge shop was part of the Toronto Shipbuilding Company's plant on Lakeshore Boulevard west of Spadina Avenue, parts of which are still standing in 1983. Built as a wartime shipyard in the first World War, it was reactivated in the second, when it built Bangor and Algerine type mine-sweepers. War supplies and munitions were manufactured in widely varying factories and workshops in Toronto, from the John Inglis plant on Strachan Avenue employing seventeen thousand workers to make Bren guns, to Casa Loma where technicians developed top secret anti-submarine devices, and even to the Laing Art Galleries on Bloor Street East, where high precision instruments were produced in the basement. Because of the war, a shortage of labour had succeeded the unemployment of the 1930s, and a new generation of women were needed in large numbers in the factories.

W. F. G. GODFREY
At Dry Dock, 1937
woodcut
25.5 x 31 cm.
MTL T13417

CAVEN ATKINS
Forge Shop, 1942
watercolour over pencil
28 x 39.4 cm.
CWM/NMM/NMC 14043

OWEN STAPLES *Lancaster over "Fair for Britain" Toronto Aug. 31st 1942*, 1943 tempera on blue-green paper 54.8 x 73.9 cm. MTL T30501 Gift of the Artist

LANCASTER OVER "FAIR FOR BRITAIN"

The Fair for Britain was sponsored by the Toronto and District Business Men's Council, with primary credit to J. W. Conklin, who set up Conklin's All-Canadian Shows in Riverdale Park. Nearly forty-three thousand dollars was raised for the *Evening Telegram* British War Victims' Fund. The Avro Lancaster was the most successful bomber of the second World War. Introduced in 1942, it was used in almost every major raid in Europe. More than four hundred were built in Canada, while twelve Royal Canadian Air Force squadrons flew them. A Lancaster has been preserved near Lakeshore Boulevard south of the Princes' Gate, given to the City by the Toronto Region, Royal Canadian Air Force Association in 1964. Staples, aged seventy-six, made watercolour sketches during the Fair, and painted this larger picture while convalescing from illness, in response to a request of the Ontario Society of Artists that its members record the spirit and accomplishment of Canada at war.

ISABEL McLAUGHLIN *Twinkle, Twinkle, Trillium*, 1945 oil on canvas 63.5 x 81.3 cm. Collection of the Artist

TWINKLE, TWINKLE TRILLIUM

The *Trillium*, built by the Polson Iron Works in 1910, is the last survivor of four large steam-powered side-paddle ferryboats that ran between Toronto and the Island. Its sister ships were the *Bluebell*, *Mayflower* and *Primrose*. Each could carry more than a thousand passengers with their bicycles, dogs, picnic baskets and other impedimenta necessary for a halcyon day on the Island. Gradually the paddle-steamers were replaced by more modern diesel boats, and in 1957 the *Trillium* was retired. She seemed fated to rot quietly away in an Island lagoon, but through the efforts of a few members of Metro Toronto Council and several interested citizens, the *Trillium* was restored and returned to service in 1976 for charters and cruises.

COLISEUM, CANADIAN NATIONAL EXHIBITION

When the Coliseum was built in 1922, it was the largest building under one roof in the world. It is used for exhibiting and judging livestock at the Canadian National Exhibition, and at the Royal Agricultural Winter Fair which was established in 1921. During the second World War, when this picture was painted, the armed forces took over the Exhibition grounds and buildings and both the Exhibition and the Fair were suspended. The Coliseum has also been used for other purposes: for example, the giant interdenominational service of thanksgiving held just before midnight on March 5, 1934, the eve of Toronto's one hundredth birthday. More than twelve thousand people, including the governor general, a choir of two thousand voices led by Dr. H. A. Fricker, civic dignitaries and distinguished men and women from all fields attended the watchnight service, and waited in the Coliseum for the beginning of Toronto's second century.

SHRINE AND SAINTS II

"I know Queen's Park pretty well," wrote Robertson Davies in 1982. "I had a pedestrian knowledge of the park, without having seen very far into its peculiar beauty. What beauty? Well, it has monuments, and although none of them is beautiful in itself, they give the park an air of being respectably furnished when they are taken in the aggregate....Certainly there is nothing of art about the likenesses of George Brown and Sir James Pliny Whitney...that flank the main entrance to the Legislature. They are simply bronze suits of Victorian formal clothes, with heads that, in Brown's case at least, greatly idealize their subjects. The statue of Oliver Mowat is nearer to the living man; for aesthetic reasons that is a pity....Nor is the statue of John Sandfield Macdonald a thing of beauty."[99]

NICHOLAS HORNYANSKY
Coliseum, Canadian National Exhibition, 194–?
pencil with watercolour and touches of gouache
32 x 24.2 cm.
MTL T10502

DAVID MILNE
Shrine and Saints II, 1943
watercolour
36.2 x 54 cm.
Hart House Permanent Collection,
University of Toronto

TOM ROBERTS *City Lights*, 1945 oil on canvas 88.9 x 109.3 cm. Collection of Mr. Maurice Nichol

CITY LIGHTS

Looking west from the old City Hall across Bay Street and a pedestrian island to Queen Street, the artist shows a typical downtown street corner during the war, when almost every man under forty and many women were in uniform. The south side of Queen Street across from the site of the present City Hall consisted mainly of pawn shops, burlesque theatres and cheap restaurants. The neon sign with the dancing girls was over the Casino, the most famous and durable of the strip-tease houses. Opened in 1936, the Casino was particularly popular during the second World War. In 1944 a delegation led by Canon W. W. Judd requested that the Police Commission close the theatre.

Calling the Casino "a notorious centre of suggestive and objectionable entertainment," Canon Judd went on, "I have a boy in the air force and he has told me one of the first things other boys ask him when they are coming to Toronto is the location of the Casino....The theatre is giving Toronto a bad name."[100] Despite such criticism, the Casino lasted for many years, although for a time it was a vaudeville house and later a legitimate theatre. In 1965, to preserve the architectural integrity of the new City Hall and Nathan Phillips Square, the City expropriated three and a half acres on the south side of Queen Street, and all the buildings were demolished.

R. YORK WILSON *Serenaders*, 1945 oil on masonite 41.4 x 57.8 cm. Collection of the Artist

SERENADERS

"Day after day you will see men under the influence of liquor, reeling through the streets or lying under the trees in the parks," wrote C. S. Clark in 1898. "Bar rooms are in full blast, and will not close until eleven."[101] Temperance societies were formed in Toronto in the 1830s, and excessive drinking – or any drinking at all – remained a vital issue in the city for more than a century. In 1877, a few months after York County voted to prohibit the sale of liquor, a vote was held in Toronto on local prohibition. The prohibitionists ("drys") built a big amphitheatre at the corner of Yonge and Queen Streets, while the "wets" held meetings in an arena on Adelaide Street. For more than two weeks, householders declared their votes publicly in the drill shed behind the City Hall; it was the last official vote in Toronto without the secret ballot. After the "wets" won by more than four to three, there was a grand torchlight procession, followed by fireworks and balloon ascensions in Queen's Park. In 1916 the provincial government introduced prohibition, which was lifted in stages beginning in 1927, when government liquor stores were established. A major change in 1947 allowed liquor to be served in cocktail bars and hotels; the following year the Prime Minister of Ontario was personally defeated in Toronto's High Park riding by a militant temperance crusader, and retired from provincial politics. This area, formerly part of the "dry" city of West Toronto, is still without liquor outlets. The painting shows a Toronto cabaret shortly before the introduction of cocktail lounges.

UNDER ST. JAMES SPIRE

"Although by no means the finest example of ecclesiastical Gothic in America," wrote Dr. Mulvany in 1884, "nor in Canada, nor, we may add, in Toronto, St. James' Church is undeniably a handsome edifice. Its best feature is the tall tower and spire." The present cathedral (Mulvany refused to use this "high-sounding foreign title") was designed by Cumberland and Storm after the destruction of its predecessor in the Great Fire of 1849. It was opened in 1853, but because of shortage of money it lacked transepts, tower, and spire. The belfry with a new peal of bells was added in 1865-66, and the spire, transepts, pinnacles, and finials in 1873-74. The illuminated clock was bought by general public subscription as "a great advantage to the citizens and strangers visiting us, and also as a beacon at night to mariners coming to our port for business and safety."[102] The unnamed lane in the foreground of the etching ran from Front Street across Colborne Street, and was used as a fish market. At least two other artists painted this view in the 1930s.

UNITED CHURCH

The Wesley Methodist (now United) Church was built on the northwest corner of Dundas Street and the present Ossington Avenue in 1874-75, and was enlarged several times, until both its width and length were doubled. It was a centre of evangelistic Methodism, with revival meetings that sometimes lasted for weeks. In 1905 its Sunday School had more than thirteen hundred pupils on the roll, making it the largest Methodist Sunday School in Canada. The church burned down in 1957. After holding services for more than three years in an abandoned popcorn factory, the congregation moved into its new church on the same site in 1961.

JAMES BLOMFIELD
Under St. James Spire, 193–?
etching
18 x 14 cm.
AO Merrilees Collection

DAVID MILNE
United Church, 1939
watercolour
37.8 x 48.6 cm.
National Gallery of Canada, Ottawa

DAVID MILNE *St. Michael's Cathedral*, 1943 colour dry-point 18.9 x 21.4 cm. AGO Gift from J.S. McLean, Canadian Fund, 1955

ST. MICHAEL'S CATHEDRAL

In the spring of 1845 the excavation for St. Michael's Cathedral was dug by volunteer labour, led by the Honourable John Elmsley in his shirt-sleeves digging with the rest. The butcher, James Wickson, donated an ox, which was roasted for thirty-six hours on the western edge of the excavation. When the ox was done, the men cut off meat to take home to their families at the end of each day's work. The earth was carted away to fill in the hollow created by Taddle Creek where it crossed Queen Street west of Sherbourne Street. Three years later the Cathedral was consecrated. Designed by William Thomas, it lacked a spire for many years, because Bishop Charbonnel believed that it was wrong to embellish the Cathedral when there were so many desperately poor people in Toronto, many of them refugees from the Irish potato famine. The tower and spire were finally built in 1866, designed by Henry Langley, who was also responsible for the dormer windows, another later addition.

JACK BUSH *Easter Processional*, 1945 oil on masonite 63 x 83.5 cm. St. Thomas' Church

EASTER PROCESSIONAL

The present St. Thomas' Anglican Church was opened in 1893 on Huron Street at Washington Avenue. At the time it was considered "the most advanced ritualistic church among all the Anglican churches of the city."[103] The earlier church building had been frequently vandalized and the congregation harassed by those who objected to Anglo-Catholicism, so that the architect, Eden Smith, a member of the congregation, placed the windows in the new church unusually high for protection against further attacks. The artist, who also belonged to the congregation, painted the solemn processional of the last wartime Easter, as the choir and banner-bearers moved through clouds of incense towards the altar. The rood screen, added in 1900, was moved to the back of the church in 1963 when the church was renovated.

PEGI NICOL MacLEOD *Jarvis Street Sidewalk*, ca 1936 watercolour 57.8 x 75.6 cm. AGO

"Jarvis is still a vibrant, living street," wrote Arnold Edinborough in 1980. "To walk along it is to feel that vibrance and to know that though it is not a neighbourhood in the sense that Cabbagetown is, it is a street of character and importance in Canadian history."[104] In the early days the lower end near the market was a busy, bustling thoroughfare. Further north were middle-class houses, while north of Carlton Street were the mansions of the rich, where families like the Cawthras, Masseys, and Gooderhams lived. Upper Jarvis Street, with its tall stately trees arching over the street, was one of the most fashionable addresses in the city from the 1870s until the 1920s when the great houses were gradually taken over by institutions or torn down. In 1946, the *Globe and Mail* reported, "During the past two decades, Jarvis Street has been deserted by many of its old and respected residents and its 13 licensed hotels, eight of them in one block, have spread its shady reputation as the heart of the city's tenderloin district far beyond Toronto's borders. In the Jarvis-Dundas area policemen patrol their beats in pairs.... Bootleggers, prostitutes and dope peddlers have made their headquarters in its big old rooming houses and apartments."[105]

JOHN S. WALSH *Chinatown, Toronto,* 1943 watercolour 37.5 x 46.4 cm. AGO

CHINATOWN, TORONTO

By 1941 there were over 2300 Chinese in Toronto, most of them in a Chinatown centred on lower Elizabeth Street and neighbouring Dundas Street. Here were the small shops selling Chinese food, clothing, household goods and bric-à-brac that were new and exotic to many Torontonians. Above the shops were little restaurants known only by their street number – 22A was a particularly good one – where anyone tired of the daily special could try eating Cantonese food with chopsticks. Behind the streets lined with shops, however, was another side of Chinatown – the little old houses scattered among Victorian factories; it was this more sombre area that Walsh painted. Much of this district was demolished in the early 1960s to make way for the new City Hall. A much larger, more prosperous Chinatown has developed west of the Art Gallery of Ontario, extending north and south of Dundas Street, as well as in a smaller area across the Don River south of Gerrard Street.

PARASKEVA CLARK
Building Clifton Road, 1947
oil on canvas
76.2 x 51.1 cm.
AGO

BUILDING CLIFTON ROAD

After the last war, Toronto again faced the problem of traffic congestion, as cars and gasoline once more became readily available. The Clifton Road extension, begun in 1947, was built from St. Clair Avenue and Mount Pleasant Road, past Clifton Road and Inglewood Drive to Jarvis and Charles Streets. Now called Mount Pleasant Road, it thus provided a badly needed new route from the northern city limits to the waterfront and was opened when construction of the subway had reduced Yonge Street to hopeless chaos. The artist is looking west across the Reservoir Creek ravine, where the road was being built, to Thornwood Road in Rosedale. Sheriff Jarvis subdivided much of his Rosedale estate in the 1850s, with large lots on long winding streets. Sir David Macpherson followed suit in the 1890s on his Chestnut Park lands north of the Jarvis property. Most of the big houses were built before the first World War, when Rosedale was succeeding Jarvis, Sherbourne and St. George Streets as Toronto's most fashionable district. The new road cut right through the heart of Rosedale, and sparked a bitter but unsuccessful fight against City Hall by local ratepayers' associations.

A SIDE LOT OF AUGUST

In the 1940s, Blomfield was often at the shop of the interior decorator, Gavin Burns, on the south side of Bloor Street east of Yonge Street, where he painted wild flower designs on chairs and other furniture. This painting of Burns' garden shows the tower of the People's Church across Bloor Street at the corner of Park Road, opened as Central Methodist Church in 1904. From his arrival in Toronto in 1920, Blomfield painted many watercolours of the city. In 1927 he said, "I hope to be known as the discoverer of Toronto."[106]

JAMES BLOMFIELD
A Side Lot of August, 1945
watercolour
27 x 38.7 cm.
AO Merrilees Collection

J.S. HALLAM *Street Market*, 1949 oil on board 47.7 x 61 cm. Mrs. J. S. Hallam

STREET MARKET

At the end of the war, Toronto was still a predominantly British city, whose citizens longed for a speedy return to ordinary living – not to the grim days of depression of the immediate pre-war years, but to the "good times" that some of them barely remembered. But Toronto was never to be the same again. Assisted by the International Refugee Organization, "displaced persons" from war-ravaged Europe arrived in thousands; with and after them came tens of thousands of immigrants from Europe, Asia and the Caribbean, bringing with them different experiences, customs and traditions. They changed the appearance of much of the city, and changed it too in many important, intangible ways. This painting shows a group of post-war immigrants at a small street market near Niagara Street.

WILLIAM A. WINTER *Midnight at Charley's*, 1945 oil on masonite 49.5 x 61 cm. Collection, the Vancouver Art Gallery

MIDNIGHT AT CHARLEY'S

There were many small cheap restaurants like this one throughout the city. Usually called by the proprietor's first name rather than by the name on their sign, they were open long hours, and were patronized by a regular, local clientele. This painting was once used by professional restaurateurs as an awful warning – "Don't let your restaurant look like this!"

SUMMER NIGHT, TORONTO

In 1885 artists were told that the "ridge which bounds the view on the north…is the only spot from which a Pisgah-like view of the entire city can be obtained, and this being the case it is surprising that its advantages have not yet been utilized."[107] Yvonne Housser painted this view from Balmoral Avenue east of Avenue Road, where she was living with Isabel McLaughlin. She shows Toronto just before the widespread development of high-rise apartment and office buildings changed its appearance and way of life. The Park Plaza Hotel on Bloor Street is almost the only tall building north of the downtown area.

SUBWAY CONSTRUCTION

Although a subway had been proposed for Toronto as early as 1880, it was not until 1946 that City Council agreed to proceed with it, a decision ratified overwhelmingly by popular vote. Toronto's first subway line was on Yonge Street between Union Station and Eglinton Avenue. It was four and a half miles long (about seven kilometres) with more than a mile above the ground. It opened in 1954, after almost five years during which some part or other of Yonge Street was completely torn up. This painting shows construction on the block north of College Street, with Eaton's College Street store in the background. The original plan had been to built the east-west subway on Queen Street, but the city's centre of gravity shifted northward, and Toronto's second subway line was built along Bloor Street and Danforth Avenue. Opened in 1966, it ran for eight miles (about thirteen kilometres) between Keele Street and Woodbine Avenue. Both the Yonge and Bloor/Danforth lines have been extended twice. In 1978 the Spadina line was opened between Downsview and St. George Street where it connected with the Yonge and Bloor/Danforth lines.

YVONNE McKAGUE HOUSSER
Summer Night, Toronto, 1949
oil on masonite
49.7 x 64.8 cm.
University of Guelph Collection
Macdonald Stewart Art Centre, Guelph, Ontario
Macdonald Institute purchase, 1956

ERIC FREIFELD
Subway Construction, 1952
watercolour
53.3 x 73.7 cm.
Toronto Transit Commission

THE CHALLENGE OF DIVERSITY/1954-1983

CHAPTER FIVE

In the 1960s and '70s Toronto became one of the fastest growing cities in North America. Downtown there was an orgy of building, upward ever upward. Subway lines were extended north, east and west. Expressways were built near the waterfront and up the Don valley; others died on the drawing board because of heated controversy about the place of the automobile in the inner city. High-rise office buildings went up at main intersections throughout the city, and high-rise apartments wherever zoning bylaws could be altered. Older working class districts like Cabbagetown were taken over by the avant-garde middle class, as white painters were succeeded by sand blasters. Yorkville became the centre of the new freedoms and life style. The city, like the suburbs, was achieving the goal of the first Chairman of Metropolitan Toronto – "to grow as large as possible as quickly as possible."[108]

In his poem, "My Two Torontos," Raymond Souster questioned this philosophy.

Now the late Sixties. What lies behind this facade
of straining skylines, expressways spewing cars,
subways where new moles ride, the very sad
high-rises, straining upward to touch the stars
or whatever lies above the black-smudge smog
smothering our lives?...[109]

An uneasy feeling was growing within the city that bigger was not necessarily better, and that the powerful developers were making too many decisions affecting the basic fabric of life. In the nineteenth century municipal reform had been concerned with social and moral issues – poverty, drunkenness, prostitution, and so on. The enemy of the new reformers was unrestricted and uncontrolled development – what the nineteenth century called progress.

For more than ten years the City of Toronto has had a reform Mayor, usually working with a fluctuating majority on Council. A new official plan, completed in 1976, emphasized the quality of life in the city and the preservation of its neighbourhoods. It encouraged projects combining office, retail and residential space, like the ManuLife Centre, and housing in the downtown area, like St. Lawrence Neighbourhood.

While Toronto struggled with the growing pains of its building boom, the city's population continued to drop. In 1982, 614,763 people lived in the city, a decrease of more than ten per cent since 1945, despite the acquisition of Forest Hill and Swansea in a reorganization of the Metropolitan system in 1967. In 1953 more than half the residents of Metropolitan Toronto lived in the city; in 1982 this had declined to slightly more than one third, although the city still has the largest population of the six municipalities in Metro.

The most significant change in the last thirty years has been in the composition of the population. From the beginning Toronto was an immigrant city; it was also overwhelmingly British in origin and tradition. By 1971, however, less than half its population was of British origin, and the proportion is steadily diminishing. Heavy immigration, mainly from Europe, the West Indies and Asia, has altered the whole character of Toronto. It has brought problems but also rewards, as old and new Torontonians adjust to the realities of the new city. In his poem, "My Toronto," J. R. C. Cermak, who came to the city as a Czech refugee in 1950, wrote,

Most change comes hard. It was so easy
when you were white and had one God,
a mighty queen in mighty England
ruling the waves, ruling the world.

That age is gone and in my time
I saw the canvas of your streets
painted with colours of all the earth.
We came to you from many lands
and learned to live in peace.
No, not in love, not in love.
But peace, too, is a thing of value...[110]

Among the newcomers were a number of artists who painted scenes of their new city. The mainstream of art in Toronto had become abstract; the influence of the Painters Eleven, formed in 1953, was very strong. There were still, however, some artists who preferred realism, and who found inspiration in the streets of Toronto. In the 1940s and '50s several painters, like William Winter and York Wilson, had portrayed life in the city, but by 1970 the emphasis was on the street – and the streetcar.

From the beginning, Toronto has been obsessed with its future. As Mayor Allan Lamport said – infelicitously but possible accurately – "Toronto is the city of the future and always will be."[111] This concern has generally kept the city on a safe, sound solid path, avoiding excess and the pitfalls of rash experiment. There have been, however, many spectacular successes and some crushing failures; there have been violent controversy and, occasionally, even more frightening unanimity. To Victorian Toronto, "progress" was the ideal, but in our own time we have seen that, uncontrolled, it can trample on tradition, compassion and humanity. This has not happened in Toronto; according to Marshall McLuhan, it is "the last great city not yet devastated by progress."[112]

"The centre of the city often presents the aspect of a building yard."[113] One of the biggest projects in Toronto's great building boom was Eaton Centre, a shopping and office complex covering three million square feet along Yonge Street from Dundas to Queen Streets. "I'm like a shipbuilder," said its architect, Eberhard Zeidler. "I build the ship; someone else sails it away."[114] The construction of Eaton Centre involved the closing of a number of streets, and lengthy negotiations with Holy Trinity Anglican Church located in the centre of the development. In this painting three historic buildings – the church, its parsonage, and the former home of Henry Scadding, the Victorian historian of Toronto and a rector of the church – stand on an island above the excavation. The Scadding house, on the left, was moved from the north to the south of the church in 1974. South of the excavation is the First Bank Tower of the Bank of Montreal's First Canadian Place (under construction behind the Simpson Tower), the old City Hall behind the Salvation Army headquarters, the CN Tower under construction, the Sheraton Centre hotel, and Eaton's warehouses on Bay Street, later demolished for the Centre. The first phase of Eaton Centre was opened in 1977, the second in 1979, and the third was approved by the City in 1982.

WALTER COUCILL
Eaton Centre Excavation, 1975
watercolour
75.5 x 100.5 cm.
Archives, Eaton's of Canada

WILLIAM ROBERTS *46 Yonge Street*, 1977 watercolour 45.7 x 30.5 cm.
The Pagurian Corporation Limited, Toronto

46 YONGE STREET

While the giant towers of the new downtown were being built, there remained a few scattered early buildings in the core of the city. A row of shops on the west side of Yonge Street south of Wellington Street still survive from the middle of the nineteenth century, and have been designated under the Ontario Heritage Act. This one on the southwest corner of Yonge and Wellington Streets probably began life as an hotel. From about 1866 to 1876 it was occupied by J.G. Joseph, at that time one of Toronto's most prominent jewellers and silversmiths. It then became the head office of the Standard Bank of Canada, until its own more impressive building was erected at Wellington and Jordan Streets in 1885, and then of the Traders' Bank until it too built a new head office. Throughout the nineteenth century, 46 Yonge Street was owned first by Sir William Howland and then by William Cawthra. In this century it has rather come down in the world, but still retains the galvanized iron window mouldings and frieze from its statelier past. When hydro poles were removed from Yonge Street in 1954, big round lights were set in the buildings.

ABA BAYEFSKY *Kiever Synagogue*, 8 April, 1959 watercolour 37.1 x 46.1 cm. MTL T10643

KIEVER SYNAGOGUE

Toronto's first synagogue (officially named Holy Blossom in 1871) was founded in 1856, when there were about 56 Jewish men in the city, most of them from England. When the great immigration of Eastern European Jews began in the 1880s, the newcomers brought with them different backgrounds, traditions, and languages; although some of them joined Holy Blossom, many banded together to form a number of small ethnic synagogues in the "Ward." The First Russian Congregation Rodfei Sholom Anshei Kiev (Kiever Synagogue) was founded in 1913 by a group that seceded from the first Russian synagogue. In 1917 it left the "Ward" and moved westward to two houses on Denison Square, just west of Kensington Market. The present synagogue was built on the site in 1923-26. Designed by Benjamin Schwartz, it is typical of the "grand period" of synagogue architecture, but on a somewhat smaller scale than other examples of this style in Toronto because the congregation was neither large nor rich. It is still used as a synagogue, and is being preserved and restored by the Toronto Jewish Congress.

In 1945, Mary Lowrey Ross said that the majority of Toronto's foreign restaurants "provide creamed salmon, chicken à la king, and cherry cup-custard, just like everybody else."[115] Angelo's, on the corner of Chestnut and Edward Streets, was an outstanding exception. Harold Town wrote that it was "dominated by the stately and haughty waitress Rosina, whose profile came from a Roman coin. During dinner hour her eyes, as they elevated from heaven to the terrazzo floor, flashed the condition of the spaghetti and the universe."[116] There had been Italians in Toronto even before it was incorporated: for example, Franco Rossi dispensed such delicacies as *parfait-amour*, wedding cake, and better ice-cream than in London, as well as copies of classical statues in Florentine alabaster, from his "ever fragrant and ambrosial"[117] shop near King and Bay Streets in 1832. The Italian community grew steadily; by 1914, half the city's fruit merchants were of Italian descent. In the last thirty years thousands of Italian immigrants have settled in Toronto, entering many business and professional fields. There are now about a quarter of a million people of Italian origin living in Metropolitan Toronto. Every one of them seemed to be on the streets when Italy won soccer's World Cup in 1982. Italian flags flew everywhere above ecstatic celebration, as Toronto went wild over the victory.

BACKYARD ON BALDWIN STREET

"To Albert Franck," wrote Harold Town, "the grubby street world of Toronto was as impressive as the pyramids at sunset or Durham Castle in the rain....Franck houses were cathedrals of the ordinary, cocoons of the humdrum, painted as seriously as if they were primal structures, essential to a full understanding of man." Town described a typical Franck painting as "a laminated conglomeration of buildings, bits added, pieces fallen away, hints of vanished fences, lean-tos, lean-froms, pushed together in an intimacy imparted in snow, a familiarity lost when the trees glutting the sky have leaves – one homogeneous lump separated by ownership, yet married by time."[118]

ALBERT FRANCK
Angelo's, 1955
oil on canvas board
61 x 50.8 cm.
Private Collection

ALBERT FRANCK
Backyard on Baldwin Street, 1964
oil on masonite
75.9 x 60.7 cm.
Rodman Hall Arts Centre, St. Catharines, Ontario
Gift of Mr. C. Bruce Hill in memory of his wife,
Charlotte Muriel Hill, 1964

CHRISTIANE PFLUG *The Squirrel*, 1967 pencil 32.3 x 25.7 cm. Estate of the Artist

THE SQUIRREL

The black squirrel, a variant of the Eastern grey squirrel, is indigenous to the Toronto area. In a 1913 list of fauna in the city and environs, they were noteworthy in High Park; now they are very common throughout the whole Metropolitan Toronto area and beyond. They have always intrigued newcomers unfamiliar with their glossy blackness: for example, Dr. G. G. Coulton, the eminent British historian who spent most of the second World War in Toronto, often described them in his letters home. "Apropos, again, the black squirrel we so amused ourselves with feeding in the summer, comes now to the window, and, unless we satisfy him at once with peanuts (he won't take crusts) gnaws at the framework. I armed that corner with a *chevaux-de-frise* of tin-tacks: but he has simply gnawed them out. Now I have plastered the place with mustard and pepper and oil, but he still gnaws at it, and the High Command of this boarding-house begins to complain seriously."[119]

ISABEL (ROWE) CLELAND *Hommage to Meryon*, 1976 dry-point etching 27.2 x 34.2 cm. Corporation of the City of Toronto

HOMMAGE TO MERYON

Two electric trolley bus routes intersect at the corner of Annette and Keele Streets, shown here from the northeast; their overhead wires create a complicated pattern above the streets. Trolley buses were first used in Toronto for a short time in the 1920s, and were reintroduced to replace streetcars on less popular routes in 1947; Toronto was then the only major North American city using them. The Toronto Transit Commission now owns one hundred and fifty trolley buses, and operates eight trolley lines. In 1983 the Commission endorsed a report recommending the phasing out of the trolleys by 1990 in favour of diesel buses, said to be cheaper to buy and to operate. Keele Street was originally a sideroad in York Township, and has always been an important thoroughfare. The Carleton Race Track, where the first four Queen's Plate races were held, was opened just west of the Keele Annette intersection in 1857. The title of this picture pays tribute to Charles Meryon, the nineteenth-century French artist who recorded Paris in his etchings.

CHRISTIANE PFLUG
Cottingham School After the Rain, 1969
oil on canvas
126.6 x 100.2 cm.
Estate of the Artist

By the early 1950s Toronto was in urgent need of more apartment and office buildings, and of more elementary schools for the children of the postwar baby boom. Cottingham Street Public School is typical of the many public schools built in the 1950s, usually surrounded by portable classrooms a short time later. The high-rise buildings in the background are also typical of the many that were built in the 1950s and 1960s, and mingle uneasily with older Toronto houses in this view south from the artist's home on Birch Avenue. After the war apartments offered a new way of life to thousands of Torontonians. It was no longer true that "living in hutches rather than houses is still largely a matter of second choice in Toronto. Apartment living has not yet become an established custom."[120] The number of apartment units in the city almost tripled between 1958 and 1966. By the 1980s the traditional house of one's own is no longer a feasible, nor even desirable, ambition for many people in Toronto, while the rapidly growing number of condominium buildings offers the apartment of one's own as another alternative.

The A & A Music store, one of Toronto's largest, is on the east side of Yonge Street across from Elm Street. This section of Yonge Street, "The Strip," has acquired an unfortunate reputation; in the last twenty years municipal politicians have occasionally campaigned to clean it up. It has had, however, unexpected defenders. In 1969 the architectural historian, Eric Arthur, wrote, "My obviously depraved taste also leads me to those areas of Toronto that can be found in all great city areas where people seem to be enjoying themselves. The Kensington Market is a perfect example, but so is Yonge Street on both sides from Dundas to Bloor. I must have a babel of tongues, and buildings must never have had their birth on a drawing board. All must be painted in the most brilliant colours – passionate purples and torrid yellows in juxtaposition are mandatory.... There never need be a dull moment on Yonge Street, or, for that matter, in Toronto. If you get to know it."[121]

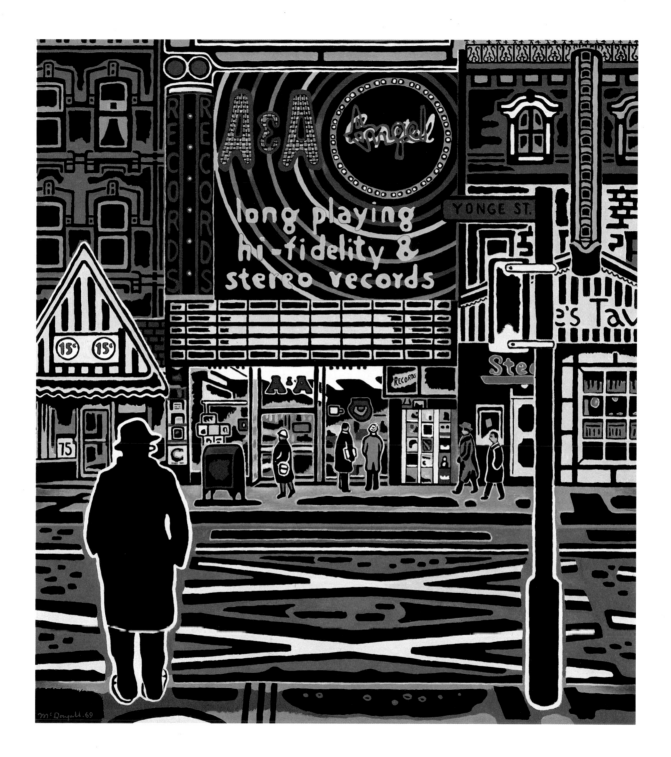

CLARK McDOUGALL
A & A Music, 1969
enamel and acrylic on board
114 x 100 cm.
Robert McLaughlin Gallery, Oshawa

ABA BAYEFSKY *Kensington Fruit Stand*, 1975 watercolour 76.2 x 56.5 cm.
Corporation of the City of Toronto

KENSINGTON FRUIT STAND

By 1912 two thirds of Toronto's Jews lived in the area bounded by Spadina, Palmerston, Queen and College. An outdoor market developed on Kensington and Augusta Avenues, and Baldwin and Nassau Streets, where chickens, fruit, clothes, etc. were displayed on barrows or stalls. Houses were gradually converted into small shops. In recent years the area has changed and the merchants in the market are now predominantly Portuguese, West Indian, Chinese, Hungarian, and Filipino, as well as Jewish. Their customers come from the downtown immigrant neighbourhoods, but also from further afield, attracted by the picturesque atmosphere, the fresh produce, and the sometimes unusual goods offered for sale.

ALBERT FRANCK *Shuter Street*, 1959 oil on canvas mounted on masonite 60 x 83.2 cm.
AGO Canada Council Joint Purchase Award, 1959

SHUTER STREET

In 1959 Shuter Street west of River Street ran through a district designated as an urban renewal area. The first major public housing project in Canada had been Regent Park, built between River and Parliament Streets from Gerrard to Dundas Streets in the late 1940s and completed in 1954. In the 1960s Regent Park South was built south of the original project between Dundas and Shuter Streets. The houses shown on the right of the painting were demolished in 1960-61 to make way for the new public housing. South of Shuter Street down to Queen Street was the Trefann Court Redevelopment Area. In 1966 City Council approved the expropriation and demolition of the roughly one hundred and fifty houses, and the relocation of over thirteen hundred people living there. About a third of the people worked, a third were on some form of pension, and a third were on welfare. Many of them objected to the City's plans, because they did not wish to move, or thought the compensation inadequate. They waged a successful battle against City Hall, assisted by a young lawyer, John Sewell, who was to be mayor of Toronto in 1979-80. Most of the houses shown in this painting on the south side of Shuter Street are still standing, as is the large building on the extreme left, now occupied by the Canadian Broadcasting Corporation.

Sunfish (now Algonquin) Island, shown here in front of part of Ward's Island, was created by the Toronto Harbour Commission during the first World War. At its eastern end is the Queen City Yacht Club, which moved to the Island in 1920. When the Island Airport was built at Hanlan's Point in 1937-38, 54 cottages displaced by the airport were floated to Algonquin Island, which was enlarged and connected with Ward's Island by a wooden bridge. In 1956 the Toronto Islands were taken over by the Municipality of Metropolitan Toronto to be part of the Metro Parks system. Leases were not renewed and many buildings were demolished to create more parkland, while the Island community fought a rearguard action to retain their homes. During the acute housing shortage after the second World War there had been twenty-two hundred people living on the Islands; but by 1981 the population had dwindled to 557 people and 252 houses, most of them on Algonquin Island and the eastern end of Ward's Island.

THE BOARD WALK AT TORONTO BEACHES

In 1907 the Toronto Street Railway Company opened the Scarborough Beach Amusement Park between Leuty and Maclean Avenues at the end of its Queen streetcar line. It included a merry-go-round, picnic facilities, refreshment stands, midway attractions, a great chute into the lake, and a lacrosse field – anyone carrying a lacrosse stick could ride free on the Company's streetcars. In 1909 the first aeroplane to fly over Toronto took off from the park. It was closed in 1925, and in 1932 the City opened a mile-long public park, including Balmy Beach, Kew Gardens and the area of the old amusement park. The boardwalk, extending from Silver Birch Avenue to Woodbine Avenue, has always been a popular resort both for people in the neighbourhood and for those from a greater distance. In 1980 the police estimated that nearly a hundred thousand people used the east end beaches on summer weekends. In this painting the artist is shown in the foreground looking west along the boardwalk from near Glen Manor Drive.

RADA GREG
Ward's Island, 1978
oil on canvas
right hand panel of triptych, each panel 50.8 x 61 cm.
Corporation of the City of Toronto

WILLIAM KURELEK
The Board Walk at Toronto Beaches, 1974
mixed media on masonite
54.6 x 43.2 cm.
Private Collection

TORONTO FROM THE PARK PLAZA

At the invitation of the World Federalists, the City of Toronto became a "World City" in 1969, and in 1972 was twinned with the City of Amsterdam. The Albert Franck Artist Exchange Programme was established in 1974 between the two cities, and the first exchange took place in 1976. In 1977, Jan Klatter, designer and set decorator with the Rotterdam Independent Theatre, came to Toronto. This sketch of the University of Toronto with a misty city beyond is strangely evocative of a Dutch rather than a Canadian city.

THE DREAM OF MAYOR CROMBIE

The artist said of this painting, "On the whole as you see this painting has a fanciful, humorous, you might say lighthearted aspect. I resorted to a dream fantasy as a gimmick to incorporate many issues and ideals into one scene....I've shown the mayor on a grassy hillside which he is doing so much to keep green. This is beautiful Glen Stewart Ravine which was back of Balsam Avenue, my home street....In his hand is his inaugural speech which I was pleased to see printed on recycled paper. At his feet is a Protest march – garbage protesting his cleanup campaign. I've used artist's licence to replace the lovely homes on Glen Manor Drive across the ravine with a housing Project for underprivileged favored by the Mayor. That's him shaking hands with the builder. You'll notice the project blends with the natural setting. This is an integral part of the central slogan of his speech, 'Renovate – Restore' towed by the helicopter labelled 'The Greening of Toronto'....Someone is said to have counted the Mayor 19 times in the picture and the Mayor himself counted himself 14 times. When I heard this out of curiosity I counted too and found 13 Crombies. In one place he's represented as an angel with white wings stopping smoke stack pollution. He's also firing warning shots at the air liner to keep quiet, but he's not seen....Two places he is Superman – where he halts the Scarborough Expressway, and stops the wreckers truck...."[122] David Crombie was mayor of Toronto from 1972 until 1978.

JAN KLATTER
Toronto overlooking University area to the south from the Park Plaza, 1977
watercolour over pencil
14.7 x 22.6 cm.
Corporation of the City of Toronto

WILLIAM KURELEK
The Dream of Mayor Crombie in Glenstewart Ravine, 1974
mixed media on masonite
79.8 x 68.6 cm.
Corporation of the City of Toronto

HUGH MACKENZIE *Survivor*, 1966 egg tempera on board 35.6 x 67.6 cm. Collection of Norcen Energy Resources Limited

SURVIVOR

After the second World War it seemed for a time that expressways would solve Toronto's rapidly increasing traffic problems. The first one to be built was the Gardiner Expressway, named after Frederick G. Gardiner, first Chairman of Metropolitan Toronto. It was intended to run along the waterfront, connecting the east and west highways into the city. There was much disagreement about its route, particularly concerning the proposal that Old Fort York be moved to the lakefront so that the expressway could cross its land. The agitation of a number of individuals and organizations, including those Gardiner called the "hysterical societies," forced the adoption of the present route around the Fort. The first section of the Gardiner Expressway was opened in 1958, and the last in 1966. Much of its seven and a half mile length (about twelve kilometres) is elevated on vast concrete piers, isolating several buildings close to the waterfront. This painting is a synthesis of the artist's impressions of the expressway and the ramps to Yonge, Bay and York Streets.

KIM ONDAATJE *Hearn Plant, Toronto Harbour*, 1974 acrylic on canvas 162 x 212 cm. D. L. McQueen

HEARN PLANT, TORONTO HARBOUR

Work began in 1949 on Ontario Hydro's new generating station south of the ship channel at the eastern end of the harbour. At that time there was an acute shortage of electric power in southern Ontario; in Toronto daily blackouts were necessary to save electricity. Named after a former general manager and chief engineer of Ontario Hydro, the Richard L. Hearn Generating Station was officially opened in 1951, with two steam generating units in operation. By 1961 it had an installed capacity of twelve hundred megawatts, with eight units fired by pulverized coal. In the 1960s the Hearn plant became Toronto's biggest single industrial polluter. A new seven-hundred-foot chimney was built in 1969-71, and the plant converted to natural gas in 1971-72 to solve the problem of pollution. The demand for electric power, however, fell far short of expectations. In 1979 the operations of the Hearn plant began to be curtailed, and in 1983 it was closed.

ARTO YUZBASIYAN *Houses, Kensington Market*, 1979 watercolour over pencil 58 x 76 cm. MTL T30072

HOUSES, KENSINGTON MARKET

This painting of Bellevue Avenue north from Denison Square shows typical downtown Toronto houses, built in the 1880s. Most of the residents in 1983 are Portuguese and Chinese. Firehall No. 8, seen on the right, was built in 1878 on the southwest corner of Bellevue Avenue and College Street. At this time, the city's firefighting service was being modernized. In the beginning fires were fought by volunteers alerted by the ringing of St. James' bell, but as the city grew, more sophisticated methods and equipment were necessary. In the 1870s six new firehalls were built and three older ones remodelled, fire alarm boxes were installed, and a permanent full-time force was established in a reorganized fire department. There were a hundred fires and fifty-six false alarms in 1879. The College Street firehall was damaged by fire in 1972, but was rebuilt according to the original design, and still serves as the fire station for a colourful part of Toronto.

ERIC FREIFELD I, *the street*, 1958-61 carbon pencil and watercolour 71.4 x 99.7 cm. Collection of Norcen Energy Resources Limited

I, THE STREET

Freifeld painted several of the big Victorian houses near his former home on Pembroke Street, giving them a distinctive air of faded grandeur and decay. The house in the foreground of this painting is based on one still standing on the northwest corner of Shuter and Sherbourne Streets. It was built in 1884-5 for a wealthy brewer, and was later occupied by a doctor and then, from 1910 to 1928, by the Rosar Funeral Home. Undertaking was originally part of the work of the cabinet-maker, who made the coffin, and the livery stable, which provided the hearse. By the 1860s undertaking was becoming a separate business. John Solleder, a German immigrant who came to Toronto from the United States, founded Toronto's oldest undertaking firm in 1861. His son-in-law, Frank Rosar, who was born in Prussia and came to Toronto from Buffalo, took over the business in 1873. The Rosar-Morrison Funeral Home is still operated by the family of its nineteenth-century founder.

JULIUS GRIFFITH *Street Corner, Yonge & Castlefield*, 1979 watercolour 57 x 78 cm. MTL T10180

YONGE & CASTLEFIELD

Yonge Street across from Castlefield Avenue is typical of many Toronto thoroughfares away from the centre of the city, lined by small two- or three-storey shops. Castlefield Avenue was originally the carriage drive to James Hervey Price's house, Castlefield, built about 1835 just east of the present Duplex Avenue. It was a striking building, no larger than an ordinary farm house, but with four miniature crenelated towers across the front between Gothic windows. There is an unsubstantiated story that the night after his defeat at Montgomery's Tavern, a short distance south, William Lyon Mackenzie hid there disguised as a baby in a cradle in the kitchen. Castlefield was bought in 1844 by Franklin Jackes, who had kept a bakery on King Street and was later elected the first warden of York County. The house was demolished in 1920.

LES TAIT "1182 Bloor St. W." 1982 watercolour 76.2 x 91.4 cm. Courtesy of Nancy Poole Studio, collection of Mr. & Mrs. J. Nelson

1182 BLOOR ST. W.

The corner grocery store has been part of Toronto life for more than a hundred years, surviving the development of supermarket and convenience store chains. Many of these stores are now kept by postwar immigrant families, who have opened up the old Victorian shops onto the sidewalks, where colourful produce is displayed in happy defiance of the Toronto winter. The storekeeper begins his day at the Ontario Food Terminal in Etobicoke; by eight o'clock each morning long processions of vans displaying advertisements in dozens of languages drive into the city with fresh fruit and vegetables. Inside his store are the crowded shelves of cans, bottles and packaged foods, much of it imported from the home country, the meat and fish counter, and a friendly meeting place for compatriots. This Portuguese store is on Bloor Street a block west of Dufferin Street. The Portuguese, many of them from the Azores, began to arrive in Toronto in the late 1950s; it is estimated that there are now more than eighty thousand in Metropolitan Toronto.

Handwritten notes on the drawing:

LAST FALL THE SUN
WAS MUCH HIGHER
& DIDN'T SHINE INTO MY
EYES AS IT IS NOW —
IT IS RIGHT BEHIND
THE UPPER PART OF
THE TOWER AT 11 A.M.
CHANGES EVERYTHING.

WHEN I SAW THE ONE WAY
TICKET TO LONDON — I
LOOKED AT THE DATE
ON MY WATCH —
THE THRILL.

RICK STANDING ON THE
TOP OF THE TOWER
WITH THE TRAP DOOR
SHUT — BETWEEN THE
LIGHTNING RODS —
MY KNEES GOT WEAK
WHEN HE TOLD ME

WHEN I REVIEWED HIS
STORY IN LONDON —
— SWEATING PALMS.

#7 Jan 17/77.

GREG CURNOE
CN *Tower #7*, 1977
pen & ink and watercolour over pencil
61 x 45.5 cm.
MTL T11783

CN TOWER #7

In the late 1960s the Canadian National and Canadian Pacific Railways were planning a joint building complex, Metro Centre, behind Union Station. At that time the rapidly increasing number of high-rise buildings in Toronto was causing difficulties for television and radio transmission; a communications tower was therefore included in the plans. When the project fell through in 1972, the Canadian National Railways agreed to build the tower separately. Designed by Malachy Grant, the CN Tower was begun in 1973 and opened in 1976. The most dramatic moment was when *Olga*, a ten-ton Sikorsky helicopter, lowered the 117-metre steel antenna onto the top. The CN Tower is the tallest free-standing structure in the world, rising 555 metres above ground level. Glass-fronted elevators take visitors to the observation deck and revolving restaurant. A large painting of the tower by Curnoe is in the National Gallery of Canada.

TORONTO FROM CENTRE ISLAND II

Like the Canadian Bank of Commerce Building a generation earlier, the Bank Tower of the Toronto-Dominion Centre soared high above the city when it was officially opened in 1968. The architectural team consisted of the Toronto firms of John B. Parkin Associates and Bregman and Hamann; the consultant was Ludwig Mies van der Rohe, one of the founding fathers of modern architecture. Because of depression and war the earlier bank building retained its supremacy for many years. The Toronto-Dominion Bank Tower's 225.5 metres above street level was soon surpassed by the West Tower (239 metres) of the Canadian Imperial Bank of Commerce complex, Commerce Court, which in turn was dominated by the First Bank Tower (285 metres) of the Bank of Montreal's First Canadian Place. As well as initiating a new scale in Toronto's downtown architecture, the Toronto-Dominion Centre also introduced extensive underground shopping malls, that now form a labyrinth of pedestrian streets under the financial heart of the city, connecting with each other and with the subway and railway transportation systems.

CHRISTIANE PFLUG
Toronto from Centre Island II, 1967
pencil
25.6 x 32.3 cm.
Estate of the Artist

MICHEL BINETTE *Brush Strokes on Dundas Street*, 1979 watercolour over pencil 51.3 x 67 cm. MTL T30076

BRUSH STROKES ON DUNDAS STREET

Toronto is one of the few remaining cities in North America where streetcars still run on its main streets. The Presidents' Conference Committee (PCC) streetcar, shown here, was first exhibited at the Canadian National Exhibition in 1938, when crowds lined up to go through the new stream-lined model. By 1953 Toronto owned more than seven hundred "red rockets," the largest fleet of PCCs in the world. In 1979-80, however, almost two hundred Canadian Light Rail Vehicles (CLRVs) went into service on Toronto streets. The new streetcar is more energy efficient than the PCC and has an improved ride, although owners of property along the streetcar lines have complained of greater noise and vibration. It is expected that the PCC streetcars will have disappeared from Toronto streets by 1984. The streetcar in the painting is shown going east on Dundas Street towards McCaul Street. The stores on the south side of Dundas Street beyond the streetcar are all Chinese.

WILLIAM KURELEK *Light Trading on the Toronto Stock Exchange*, 1973 mixed media on masonite
91.4 x 109.2 cm. Loewen, Ondaatje, McCutcheon & Company Limited, Toronto

TORONTO STOCK EXCHANGE

The Toronto Stock Exchange was founded in 1852 with twelve members, each paying five dollars for membership and trading in each others' offices. In 1861, when it began to issue authorized stock lists to the newspapers, it traded in only thirty-six issues. The Exchange grew with the country, reflecting its economic development, although for many years it refused to be involved with mining stock which it considered too speculative. Two rival mining exchanges were established in the 1890s, which amalgamated in 1899 to form the Standard Stock and Mining Exchange. After the Ontario government forced a merger of the Toronto and Standard exchanges in 1934, a new building was necessary for their combined operations. Opened on Bay Street in 1937, it was designed by George and Moorhouse with S. H. Maw as associate, and was regarded as the most modern exchange building in the world. It was said to be the only completely air-conditioned building in Canada. Traders employed by members of the Exchange shouted offers to buy and sell on the trading floor, shown here, with its nine hexagonal posts for trading. High on the walls, just visible on the right, were eight large murals by Charles Comfort, who also designed the frieze along the building's facade; both represent Canada's major industries. In 1982 the Toronto Stock Exchange traded more than one and a half billion shares worth close to eighteen billion dollars; it is the third largest stock exchange in North America and the fifth in the world. It is also the only stock exchange in the world to trade in stocks, options and futures. In 1983 the Toronto Stock Exchange moved to much larger, consolidated quarters in First Canadian Place.

RAYMOND CHOW
Long Lilliput Look, 1977
acrylic on canvas
70.8 x 71 cm.
MTL T10419

LONG LILLIPUT LOOK

This view from the Island shows the Harbour Castle in front of the CN Tower, the Toronto Star building, the Royal York Hotel, the Toronto-Dominion Centre, the First Bank Tower of First Canadian Place, and the West Tower of Commerce Court. The Toronto Hilton Harbour Castle was only one of eight major hotels opened in the city in 1975. Toronto had experienced a shortage of hotel rooms; it also hoped to expand its role as a major North American convention centre.

QUEEN 1977/8

Art was first introduced into Toronto's subway stations on the Spadina line, opened in 1978. After the Spadina artists were chosen, the Robert Simpson Company Ltd., Eaton's of Canada, the Eaton Centre, and Wintario sponsored a competition for a mural to be donated by them and placed in the Queen subway station. One of the conditions of the competition was that the design include Simpson's store, the Eaton Centre and the City Hall. Boyle's winning maquette differs from his mural, "Our Nell," installed in the station in 1980, most notably in the portrait of William Lyon Mackenzie. The woman is Nellie McClung, the Western Canadian writer and suffragette.

KING SUBWAY STATION

"Although the generally spick-and-span appearance and the efficiency of the older subway lines and stations have been praised by visitors from all over the world," wrote Bruce West, "those stations do now look a bit sterile and utilitarian in an era when the mood seems to be to provide more eye appeal to such public places. As one disappointed Toronto artist rather bitterly remarked, after the Spadina art project appeared to have become bogged down, 'Unless you treat the subway as your own home, it becomes a public urinal and a place to get stabbed in.' "[123] King is one of the busiest stations during rush hours, when thousands of people pour through its corridors on their way to and from their offices in the sky.

(above)
JOHN BOYLE
Queen 1977/8, 1977-78
acrylic on board
14.2 x 76 cm.
Corporation of the City of Toronto

(below)
BRIAN KIPPING
King Subway Station, 1983
oil on wood
19.1 x 35.6 cm.
Bau-Xi Gallery

ROD PROUSE *Santa Claus Parade*, 1977 pastel, watercolour & pencil 51 x 66.7 cm. MTL T13236

SANTA CLAUS PARADE

On December 3, 1905, Santa Claus arrived in Toronto by train, and circled several city blocks before going to Eaton's department store. Eaton's continued to sponsor the annual Santa Claus parade until 1982, when it became a co-operative effort co-ordinated by the Metropolitan Toronto government. In the early years Santa Claus travelled almost alone, but in 1918 he was joined by Mother Goose and Cinderella. From then on, all the favourite characters in nursery rhymes and fairy tales appeared in the parade, as well as more contemporary characters like Andy Gump in 1926, and the Muppets in 1981.

The 1913 parade included eight reindeer borrowed from the missionary and explorer Sir Wilfred Grenfell, but the experiment was not completely successful because the animals became nervous in the crowded streets. In 1981 there were about sixteen hundred people in the parade, watched by an estimated half million on Toronto streets, and by thirty million television viewers in Canada and the United States. The painting shows the parade passing the Park Plaza Hotel and the Church of the Redeemer at the corner of Avenue Road and Bloor Street.

CARLOS MARCHIORI *Bloor Street West*, 1976 acrylic on board 60.9 x 76.3 cm. MTL T10151

"Bloor and Yonge, a valve for movement. A portal to pleasure. A centre for sundry city activity. Two blocks of the slickest cash registers in town. Many things to many people. The Corner, however, is for certain people one thing more. It is for them plain and simple the centre of the universe."[124] When John Reeves wrote of the "Big Corner" in 1972, several tall buildings were under construction near the corner. In this painting, Stollery's store on the southwest corner is dwarfed by the ManuLife Centre further west, and by the Holt Renfrew, Canadian Imperial Bank of Commerce, and Hudson's Bay Company buildings on the north side of Bloor Street. In 1923 J. E. Middleton described Stollery's men's store as "a splendid modern building which is a notable example of architectural art applied to the problems of providing adequate housing for business enterprises of magnitude."[125] When Bloor Street was widened in 1929, however, half the store had to be torn down.

SATURDAY AFTERNOON MATINEE

Unlike most of the downtown movie theatres, the Eglinton Theatre, just west of Avenue Road, was built as a cinema rather than having been converted from use for plays or vaudeville. Unlike them also, it has not been modernized nor cut up into a number of smaller auditoriums, so that its art deco interior, shown here, is still intact. Designed by Kaplan and Sprachman, it opened in 1937, when its interior won the bronze medal of the Toronto Chapter of the Ontario Association of Architects. Going to the Saturday afternoon matinée was a tradition for Toronto's young people for many years. When the Eglinton Theatre was built, the feature film with movie stars like Shirley Temple, Mickey Rooney, or Judy Garland, was accompanied by trailers of forthcoming movies, a news short, a cartoon comedy and a chapter of a serial usually set either in the West or in space but always with a cliff-hanger ending. The audience happily gasped, booed and cheered throughout the serial. It also expressed its opinions during the news: for example, appearances of members of the royal family were always applauded by Toronto audiences.

ISLANDS OFF THE LAKE

Standing on the Gardiner Expressway at dawn, the artist looks down on the complicated intersection of Parkside Drive and the Lakeshore Boulevard with the lake beyond. The Sunnyside Bathing Pavilion is just to the west; this whole area was the site of the Sunnyside Amusement Park until 1956. On the other side of the expressway is High Park, John G. Howard's magnificent gift to Toronto in 1873. In return for an annuity for himself and his wife (they were both in their seventies at the time), he gave the city 165 acres for use as a park. The city later bought 241 acres of adjacent land, so that High Park is one of the largest parks within the city of Toronto. One of its attractions is Howard's old home, Colborne Lodge, now a beautifully preserved museum in the care of the Toronto Historical Board. During the summer many of Howard's watercolours hang in the gallery in Howard's old coach house, as well as in the house itself.

GERALD LAZARE
Study for Saturday Afternoon Matinée, 1978
charcoal and pencil
45.8 x 36.6 cm.
MTL T12929

GERALD ZELDIN
Islands off the Lake, 1977
pastel, ink, gouache, on brown paper
50.2 x 64.8 cm.
Corporation of the City of Toronto

RAYKA KUPESIC *Winter on Nathan Phillips Square*, 1982 oil on canvas 37.7 x 61 cm.
Private Collection

E. J. Lennox's monumental City Hall at the head of lower Bay Street, which had seemed so huge in 1900, was filled to – and beyond – capacity by the 1950s. Municipal government was rapidly growing in both size and complexity, and was further complicated by the formation of the Municipality of Metropolitan Toronto. Nathan Phillips, the city's "Mayor of all the people" from 1955 to 1962, passionately believed that "Toronto deserved the finest City Hall and Civic Square in the world."[126] Voters rejected the building of a new City Hall in 1955, but in the 1956 election the proposal was approved. An international architectural competition supervised by Eric Arthur resulted in submissions from over five hundred architects from forty-two countries, and was won by Viljo Revell of Finland, who chose John B. and John C. Parkin as his Toronto associates. The first sod was turned in 1961, and the new City Hall was opened in 1965. Eric Arthur wrote, "Taller buildings will be built before the end of the century here and elsewhere in North America, but there will be no comparable, or no more renowned city hall."[127]

JOHN WARD *Sunset on King Street*, 1981 acrylic on board 38.1 x 35.6 cm.
Private Collection

SUNSET ON KING STREET

The artist writes, "I am interested in the notion of change and the passing of time. In my own life I feel like a witness, a visitor passing through. In 1981, when I painted this picture I had occasion to be on King Street on a regular basis. One evening I looked up at the old and new buildings set against the sky. The juxtaposition of the old and the new reaffirmed a sense of continuation."[128] This view of King Street is from George Street, the western edge of Simcoe's original settlement. In 1834 this was the heart of Toronto, with the market, the largest church, and the most important places of business. In 1983 it is a symbol of Toronto's history. Here are St. Lawrence Hall (1851), St. James' Cathedral (1853; spire 1874), the Canadian Bank of Commerce building (1931), the West Tower of Commerce Court (1974), and the First Bank Tower of First Canadian Place (1976). Here past and present stand side by side, visible evidence of the city's one hundred and fifty years.

FOOTNOTES

1 *Colonial Advocate*, Toronto, 1 Feb. 1827

2 *Courier of Upper Canada*, Toronto, 27 Oct. 1832, quoting from the Kingston *Patriot*

3 AO, Sir Sandford Fleming, Diary, 17-31 Oct. 1851

4 *Patriot*, Toronto, 4 July 1834

5 *British Colonist*, Toronto, 1 Oct. 1850

6 J. G. Kohl, *Travels in Canada*, trans. by Mrs. Percy Sinnett, London, 1861, II p. 16

7 John Walter, *First Impressions of America*, London, 1867, p.42

8 Sir W. H. Russell, *Canada; its Defences, Condition and Resources*, London, 1865, p.52

9 J. F. Campbell, *A Short American Tramp in the Fall of 1864*, Edinburgh, 1865, p.251

10 Mrs. Anna Jameson, *Winter Studies and Summer Rambles in Canada*, London, 1838, I p.2

11 Walter Henry, *Trifles from my Port-folio*, Quebec, 1839, p.110

12 Jameson, *Winter Studies and Summer Rambles*, I p.2

13 AO, Thomas Glegg, Sketch Book, Note Book

14 MTL, Ensign A. C. Robertson, Diary 1837-1841, II p.99

15 *British Colonist*, Toronto, 1 Oct. 1850

16 AO, Mrs. Mary O'Brien, Journals, 3 Feb. 1829

17 *Toronto Herald*, 30 Dec. 1841

18 MTL, Powell Papers, Mrs. S. P. Jarvis to W. D. Powell, 5 March 1828

19 Ibid., Mrs. W. D. Powell to George Murray, 15 Jan. 1832

20 MTL, J. G. Howard Papers, Section III, 1368

21 *Globe*, Toronto, 13 Nov. 1851

22 MTL, Toronto Mechanics' Institute Papers, unbd., G. F. Price to Committee of Judges, Sept. 1851

23 A. W. H. Rose, *The Emigrant Churchman in Canada by the Rev. Henry Christmas*, London, 1849, I p. 84

24 *British Colonist*, Toronto, 27 June 1845

25 Ure, G. P., *The Hand-book of Toronto*, Toronto, 1858, p.198

26 University of Toronto, Archives, H. H. Langton Papers, John Langton to William Langton, 12 Nov. 1856

27 Henry Scadding, *Toronto of Old*, Toronto, 1873, p.313

28 Eric Arthur, *Toronto, No Mean City*, Toronto, 1974, p.103

29 MTL, J. G. Howard Diaries, 9 March 1848

30 *Toronto Mirror*, 22 June 1855

31 AO, Thomas Glegg, Sketch Book, Note Book

32 John Imrie, "Toronto," in his *Sacred Songs, Sonnets and Miscellaneous Poems*, Toronto, 1886, p.54

33 Lucius O'Brien to Robert Harris, 14 Aug. 1879, quoted in Moncrieff Williamson, *Robert Harris 1849-1919, an Unconventional Biography*, Toronto, 1970, p.60-61

34 Quoted in ibid., p.73, 74, 62-63

35 C. C. Taylor, *Toronto "Called Back" from 1886 to 1850*, Toronto, 1886, p. 240-41

36 C. S. Clark, *Of Toronto the Good*, Montreal, 1898, p.1

37 *Toronto Illustrated*, 1893, p.17

38 W. J. Loudon, *Studies Of Student Life*, V, Toronto, 1928, p.34-35

39 Joseph Jackes to James Jackes, Sept. 1874, and Joseph Jackes to J. H. Price, May, 1865, quoted in L. B. Martyn, *Aristocratic Toronto: 19th Century Grandeur*, Toronto, 1980, p.67, 66

40 *Bystander*, Jan. 1881, p.19

41 Dennis Reid, "Our Own Country Canada," Ottawa, 1979, p.302

42 C. S. Clark, *Of Toronto the Good*, Montreal, 1898, p.81-82

43 Quoted in Williamson, *Robert Harris*, p.72

44 Walt Whitman, "Diary in Canada," in his *Daybooks and Notebooks*, III, New York, 1978, p.626, 627

45 G. Mercer Adam, *Toronto, Old and New*, Toronto, 1891, p.51

46 MTL, W. W. Baldwin Papers II, J. S. Baldwin to Laurent Quetton de St. George, 8 Aug. 1817

47 *Toronto Star*, 6 Feb. 1926

48 G. M. Adam, *Toronto, Old and New*, Toronto, 1891, p.49

49 *Globe*, Toronto, 3 Dec. 1883

50 C. P. Mulvany, *Toronto: Past and Present*, Toronto, 1884, p.144-45

51 Arnold Brown, "What Hath God Wrought?" 2d ed., Toronto, 1957, p.21

52 Karl Baedeker, *The Dominion of Canada*, Leipzig, 1900, p.166

53 G. M. Grant, ed., *Picturesque Canada*, Toronto, 1882, I p.407

54 *History of Toronto and the County of York, Ontario*, Toronto, 1885, I p.298

55 Henry Scadding and J.C. Dent, *Toronto: Past and Present: Historical and Descriptive*, Toronto, 1884, p.314

56 Ibid., p.315

57 A. E. Copping, *Canada Today and Tomorrow*, London, 1911, p.76-77

58 A. B. Garvin, *Toronto, Romance of a Great City* by Katherine Hale, Toronto, 1956, p.208

59 Lawren Harris, *The Story of the Group of Seven*, Toronto, 1964, p.14

60 Ibid., p. 26-27

61 Quoted in *Toronto between the Wars, a Portfolio*, Toronto, 1971

62 Jan Morris, *Travels*, London, 1976, p.59

63 J. E. Middleton, *The Municipality of Toronto, a History*, Toronto, 1923, I p.405

64 Lilian Whiting, *Canada, the Spellbinder*, London, 1917, p.87

65 *Globe*, Toronto, 20 Nov. 1914

66 *Patriot*, Toronto, 12 Sept. 1837

67 *My Toronto*, Toronto, 1970, p.53-54

68 MTL, Alice M. Keys, "Not 'The Beaches'" typescript, 197-?

69 *Illustrated Historical Atlas of the County of York*, Toronto, 1878, p. xiii

70 Mazo de la Roche, *Ringing the Changes, an Autobiography*, Toronto, 1957, p.66-67

71 M. H. Irish, Imperial Munitions Board, to Lt. Col. E.J. Chambers, Chief Press Censor, 27 Oct. 1916, quoted in Barbara Wilson, *Ontario and the First World War, 1914-1918*, Toronto, 1977, p.103

72 J. E. Middleton, *The Municipality of Toronto, a History*, Toronto, 1923, I p.386

73 *Globe*, Toronto, 27 Aug. 1915

74 Lawren Harris, *The Story of the Group of Seven*, Toronto, 1964, p.14

75 *Toronto Star*, 12 June 1919

76 *History of Toronto and the County of York, Ontario*, Toronto, 1885, I p.284

77 *Globe*, Toronto, 21 March 1922

78 *Telegram*, Toronto, 6 April 1922

79 Lawren Harris, *Contrasts, a Book of Verse*, Toronto, 1922, p.57

80 Jeremy Adamson, *Lawren S. Harris, Urban Scenes and Wilderness Landscapes, 1900-1930*, Toronto, 1973, p.118

81 Harry Gairey, *A Black Man's Toronto, 1914-1980*, Toronto, 1981, p.8

82 Archives, AGO, Lawren Harris to Sydney Key, 20 July 1948

83 J. E. Middleton, *The Municipality of Toronto, a History*, Toronto, 1923, I p.402

84 Bill Ross, Jr., quoted in Albert Tucker, *Steam into Wilderness*, Toronto, 1978, p.103

85 Quoted in *Toronto between the Wars, a Portfolio*, Toronto, 1971

86 Hubert [i.e. Hugh] Garner, "Toronto's Cabbagetown," *Canadian Forum*, June 1936, p.14

87 Paraskeva Clark, "Come Out From Behind the Pre-Cambrian Shield," *New Frontier*, April 1937, p.16-17

88 National Film Board, *Portrait of the Artist as an Old Lady*, quoted in *Toronto Star*, 29 Jan. 1983

89 David Milne to Mr. and Mrs. Vincent Massey, July 1940, quoted in Marlborough Godard, *David Milne, the Toronto Year, 1939-1940*, Toronto, 1976, p.10

90 David Milne, Jr., in ibid., p.10

91 Pierre Berton, *The New City, a Prejudiced View of Toronto*, Toronto, 1961, p.57

92 Stephen Leacock, "A Tale of Two Cities," *Maclean's Magazine*, 1 March 1943, p.7-8

93 C. P. Mulvany, *Toronto: Past and Present*, Toronto, 1884, p.44

94 *Toronto Star*, 8 Oct. 1965

95 J. E. Middleton, *Toronto's 100 Years*, Toronto, 1934, p.1

96 J. G. Langton, quoted in ibid., p.145-46

97 Letter from Carl Schaefer, 17 Dec. 1972

98 Morley Callaghan, *It's Never Over*, Toronto, 1930, p.3-5

99 Robertson Davies, "Queen's Park," *Toronto Life*, April 1982, p.58

100 Quoted by Cec Jennings, *Globe and Mail*, Toronto, 27 Feb. 1980

101 C. S. Clark, *Of Toronto the Good*, Montreal, 1898, p.143-44

102 W. H. Pearson, *Recollections and Records of Toronto of Old*, Toronto, 1914, p.263

103 J. Ross Robertson, *Landmarks of Toronto*, IV, Toronto, 1904, p.73

104 Foreword to Austin Seton Thompson's *Jarvis Street, a Story of Triumph and Tragedy*, Toronto, 1980, p. x

105 *Globe and Mail*, Toronto, 21 Dec. 1946

106 Quoted in Gertrude Pringle, "James Blomfield, Water-Color Painter," *Willisons Monthly*, Sept. 1927, p.134

107 *History of Toronto and the County of York, Ontario*, Toronto, 1885, I p.284

108 Frederick G. Gardiner, Minutes, Metropolitan Toronto Council, 1955, Appendix C, p.3

109 Raymond Souster, "My Two Torontos," *Habitat* 10, no. 3-6, 1967, p.75

110 J. R. C. Cermak, "My Toronto," manuscript

111 Quoted in J. R. Colombo, "A Lampy Sampler," *Toronto Star*, "The City," 9 April 1978

112 Quoted in E.A. Starbird, "Canada's Dowager Learns to Swing," *National Geographic*, Aug. 1975, p.209

113 Eugène Cloutier, *No Passport, a Discovery of Canada*, trans. by Joyce Marshall, Toronto, 1968, p.268

114 Quoted in Leon Whiteson, *The Liveable City*, Oakville, 1982, p.15

115 M. L. Ross, "Be-kind-to-Toronto Week Might Do the Patient a Lot of Good," *Saturday Night*, 3 Feb. 1945, p.9

116 Harold Town, *Albert Franck, Keeper of the Lanes*, Toronto, 1974, p.19

117 Henry Scadding, *Toronto of Old*, Toronto, 1873, p.94

118 Harold Town, *Albert Franck, Keeper of the Lanes*, Toronto, 1974, p.24, 28

119 Quoted in Mary Coulton, *Father, a Portrait of G. G. Coulton at Home* by Sarah Campion, London, 1948, p.186

120 Martin Loeb, quoted in Pierre Berton, *The New City, a Prejudiced View of Toronto*, Toronto, 1961, p.29

121 *My Toronto*, Toronto, 1970, p.49-50

122 City of Toronto Archives, excerpts from talk by William Kurelek

123 Bruce West, *Toronto*, Toronto, 1979, p.258-59

124 John Reeves, "Stories of the Big Corner, Yonge and Bloor," *Toronto Life*, Sept. 1972, p.33

125 J. E. Middleton, *The Municipality of Toronto, a History*, Toronto, 1923, II p.43

126 Nathan Phillips, *Mayor of All the People*, Toronto, 1967, p.140

127 Eric Arthur, *Toronto, No Mean City*, Toronto, 1974, p.236

128 Letter from John Ward to author, 19 Jan. 1983

PHOTOGRAPHY CREDITS

AEAC, 51;   AGO, 59, 71, 100, 102, 107, 112, 118, 124, 130-32,134, 150, 152-54, 173;   AO, 16, 21, 30, 37, 70, 148, 155;   Archives of the United Church of Canada, 24;   Beaverbrook Art Gallery, Fredericton, 116;   CWM/NMM/NMC, 104, 105, 108-11, 141;   City Photographer, City of Toronto, 15, 18, 39, 63, 64, 66, 85, 87, 88, 98, 125, 136, 137, 146, 169, 172, 174, 176, 189 (above), 193;   MTL, 17, 20, 29, 32, 33, 36, 40, 41, 45, 48, 49, 54, 56, 61, 65, 69, 72, 81, 82, 84, 91, 96, 97, 101, 113, 140, 142, 144, 165, 180, 182, 188, 192;   Macdonald Stewart Art Centre, University of Guelph, 158;   National Gallery of Canada, 43, 120, 121, 149;   PAC, 25, 28, 77;   ROM, 12, 19, 26, 31, 50, 76, 117;   TBE, 80;   Toronto Transit Commission, 159;   Vancouver Art Gallery, 157

James A. Chambers, 14, 22, 23, 34, 35, 38, 42, 44, 46, 57, 58, 62, 67, 68, 73, 78, 79, 83, 86, 90, 94, 106, 128, 135, 138, 139, 151, 156, 164, 168, 175, 178, 179, 181, 184-86, 190, 191, 195;   Hans Geerling, 187;   Sherman Hines, 99, 103, 119;   T.E. Moore, 2, 89, 123, 147, 171, 177, 194;   Michael Neill, 166, 167;   Herb Nott, 133, 143;   Norm Scudellari, 114, 162;   Lois Steen, 122;   TDF Artists Ltd., 145;   Ron Vickers, 74, 170;   Helena Wilson, 183, 189 (below)

Jack Bush paintings reproduced courtesy The Estate of Jack Bush ©reserved
David Milne paintings reproduced courtesy The Estate of David Milne ©reserved

ABBREVIATIONS

AEAC	Agnes Etherington Art Centre, Queen's University, Kingston
AGO	Art Gallery of Ontario, Toronto
AO	Archives of Ontario, Toronto
CWM/NMM/NMC	Canadian War Museum/National Museum of Man/National Museums of Canada, Ottawa
MTL	Metropolitan Toronto Library
MTL JRR	Metropolitan Toronto Library, J. Ross Robertson Collection
OHF	Ontario Heritage Foundation
PAC	Public Archives of Canada, Ottawa
ROM CC	Royal Ontario Museum, Toronto, Canadiana Collection
ROM DE	Royal Ontario Museum, Toronto, Department of Ethnology
ROM SS	Royal Ontario Museum, Toronto, Sigmund Samuel Collection
TBE	Toronto Board of Education
THB	Toronto Historical Board

INDEX OF ARTISTS

INDEX OF PICTURES